Art Matters

Art Matters

Strategies, Ideas, and Activities to
Strengthen Learning across the Curriculum

Eileen S. Prince

Zephyr Press

Tucson, Arizona

Art Matters:
Strategies, Ideas, and Activities to Strengthen Learning across the Curriculum

Grades K–12

ISBN 1-56976-129-9

Editor: Kirsteen E. Anderson
Design and Production: Daniel Miedaner
Illustrations: Eileen S. Prince and students at Sycamore School
Cover: Daniel Miedaner

Publisher:
Zephyr Press
P.O. Box 66006
Tucson, Arizona 87528-6006
800-232-2187
www.zephyrpress.com
www.i-home-school.com

Library of Congress Cataloging-in-Publication Data

Prince, Eileen S., 1947-
    Art matters : strategies, ideas, and activities to strengthen learning across the
curriculum / Eileen S. Prince.
       p. cm.
    Includes bibliographical references and index.
    ISBN 1-56976-129-9 (alk. paper)
    1   Art—Study and teaching (Elementary)—United States. 2. Art—Study and teaching
(Secondary)—United States. 3. Art in education—United States. I. Title.

N362 .P75 2001
707'.1'273—dc21   2001017718

Acknowledgments

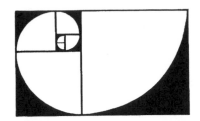

I would like to express my deep appreciation to Dr. Nyle Kardatzke and all the parents, students, staff, administrators, and faculty of Sycamore School for their support and inspiration. Art teachers rarely receive the kind of encouragement and respect you have granted me over the years, and I am truly grateful.

Special thanks also go to:

- Paula Fair, music teacher par excellence, for her many contributions, enlightening conversations, and outstanding example as an educator

- Paula Jurgonski, a superb math teacher whose love of her subject is contagious and who introduced me to some great sources

- Sue Vieth, a wonderful teacher and role model, for taking time from her many fourth-grade duties to supply me with helpful references

- Larry Fletcher, computer guru, for his unfailing good humor and assistance

- Betty Krebs and Russ Blanford, whose help in a variety of ways has contributed to my ability to teach

- All the teachers, past and present, with whom I have worked and from whom I have learned

- Susan Longhenry and other staff members at the Indianapolis Museum of Art

- Veronica Durie, at Zephyr Press, for her indispensable help and suggestions

- Dan Miedaner, for his patience and graphic expertise

- Kirsteen Anderson, for her brilliant editing

- Barbara Freeman, for her years of free therapy and hours of help on this volume

- Donna Segal, for free professional consulting

And most importantly I thank my family, who continue to be my best teachers: my mom; my wonderful husband, Irwin, whose support has allowed me to do what I love; and my terrific sons, Ben and Josh, for being extremely easy to raise and giving me so much joy. Your wit and wisdom never cease to delight me. To all the rest of the family as well, thanks for your encouragement throughout the years. ❧

Contents

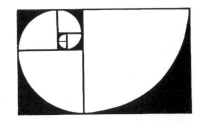

Introduction

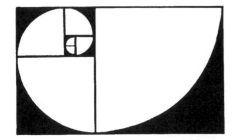

"A room hung with pictures is a room hung with thoughts."
—Sir Joshua Reynolds, 1723–1792

Recently, a student of mine wrote that she could remember almost any fact if she had an image to associate with it. That concept alone—that some students learn best visually—should offer reason enough to support integrating art more forcefully into the general curriculum. Art has a tremendous capacity to engage students, offering science, history, math, social studies, and literature teachers an alternative way to reach their pupils. In the best schools, art specialists work reciprocally with instructors in other disciplines to support each other's content. History teachers use art to illuminate important events or trends while art teachers correlate works to historical eras and various cultures. Science classes may study the physics of light while art classes focus on its consequences to color. Unfortunately, few teachers on either side of this potentially wonderful partnership are fully aware of its possibilities. Because schools historically have downplayed the arts—or removed them altogether—most teachers of other subjects have little or no personal background in this area. You may find it hard to believe that virtually all teachers can use art to enhance their classes. "Not me," you may say. "I can't draw a straight line!" Conversely, art specialists are frequently unaware of the terrific opportunities they have to teach science, math, or literature. Yet, as I hope to show in this book, the common ground among the various disciplines is so vast, and the possibilities for interaction so plentiful and varied, any teacher of any course should find countless ways to integrate multiple subjects productively.

The Nature of Art Education

Since many of you are probably more familiar with the "pumpkins-in-October, turkeys-in-November" variety of art class than what is commonly called "discipline-based art education," I would like to describe what I mean by "teaching art." Several times a year, I receive notices for new publications designed to help me "teach art." Many of these materials are quite useful, and over the years some wonderful programs have been developed. Unfortunately, however, I still receive too many letters that start out with "Looking for lesson plans?" or "Need something to do in your classroom?" and then offer me 365 "things to do on rainy days" that are guaranteed to keep my students occupied with hands-on activities. The implications of such an approach infuriate me. I imagine the marketing department sitting around a table saying:

> You know, those art teachers have nothing to do with their time. After all, art class is just a frill, a time for students to get some much-needed rest from the intellectual demands of the school day by doing some fun cut-and-paste. Since they have no real content of their own, art teachers must find it tough to come up with endless projects to keep the little tykes quiet during this down time.

I do not know which makes me angrier, the insult to the intelligence and curricula of all the terrific art teachers out there, or the fact that in far too many cases, art teachers are not only not insulted by this approach, but downright grateful for it. The alternative scenario is even more frightening and culturally significant. In it the marketers take note of the fact that in more and more schools, trained art teachers are being cut from the staff (or were never part of it to begin with) and classroom teachers are being required to include art instruction in the course of their other duties. Since these teachers rarely have significant background in art, and since they are usually pressed for time to teach all the content they were trained for, they frequently are in need of prepackaged lesson plans to help them keep some semblance of sanity.

I have nothing against prepackaged art lessons per se. Like any teacher, I am constantly looking for improved and more efficient ways to teach my subject,

> Art has never been a purely visual exercise. Although my response to a work may be intensely aesthetic, it will always have an emotional or intellectual component. The best art will engage me on all three levels— aesthetic, emotional, and intellectual. From the creator's point of view as well, art is an intellectual exercise. It requires constant decision making, no matter how subconscious those decisions might be.

so I am always thankful for valid resources that can help me do a better job. The poor quality of the projects generally promoted by such means may offend me, but I am even more offended at the underlying message such a marketing strategy conveys. It portrays a visual arts curriculum as a random collection of cookie-cutter projects devoid of intellectual content, fundamental rationale, or higher-order thinking. Do math teachers get mailings like this? Do science teachers?

I believe strongly that art requires intelligence. Indeed, in his recent book *Life: The Movie,* cultural historian Neal Gabler suggests that one of the primary differences between art and entertainment is that a work of art requires some sort of intellectual effort on the part of the viewer. Art has never been a purely visual exercise. Although my response to a work may be intensely aesthetic, it will always have an emotional or intellectual component. The best art will engage me on all three levels—aesthetic, emotional, and rational. From the creator's point of view as well, art is an intellectual exercise. It requires constant decision making, no matter how subconscious those decisions might be. It requires superior observation skills, the ability to process information and then apply it in unique ways and, perhaps most importantly, something of substance to communicate. The broader the intellectual education and understanding of the artist, the greater the chance that he or she will find the universal themes and insights common to great art. Michelangelo recognized the intellectual component of art when he wrote, "A man paints with his brains and not with his hands." And Richard L. Anderson, in his wonderful book *Calliope's Sisters,* states that the artist's special abilities are more often mental than manual.

Figure 1. A structured art curriculum enhances creativity, encouraging students to look at subjects in a wide variety of ways and choose interpretations that are meaningful to them.

Similarly, a valid art curriculum has substance and is intellectually stimulating. It presents significant content and continuously develops students' problem-solving skills. It requires constant decision making, demands high standards of achievement, and instills in students a deep respect for art as a discipline. It accommodates all learning styles and is self-individualizing (see figure 1). It promotes intellectual honesty and curiosity, and it encourages diversity. It discourages judgments based upon ignorance and prejudice. It honors excellence. The content and methodology found in a quality art class are parallel to the substance and structure of any other well-taught discipline. Only when teachers, administrators, and parents recognize this fact will they acknowledge the value and importance—and indeed, the wonderful possibilities—of using art to enhance the curriculum.

The Importance of Art Education

We live in an era when many believe "high" art is becoming increasingly difficult for the average person to comprehend. We have unrestricted right of entry to museums and galleries, but our fundamental access to these venues is limited by our inability to relate to the art we find there. At the same time, "low" or commercial art permeates every facet of our lives. One way or another, we are constantly being addressed in the "language" of art, and anyone who fails to study that language will miss a lot of information. The study of art, like the study of any language, involves learning vocabulary and syntax, idiom, and nuance. We must try to think in the language, to "immerse" ourselves in a society that speaks that native tongue. The more fluent we become in the language of art, the more it can tell us about our society, about our world, about history, and most importantly perhaps, about ourselves.

> *"An ulcer is an unkissed imagination, an undanced dance, an unpainted painting."*
> —Don Giardi

At a convention several years ago, I heard Eliott Eisner speak of art as an alternative way of knowing the world, and teachers are certainly aware that many students' primary means of interpreting classroom material is through visual input. For some people, the language of art is also the best method of communicating what they want to tell us, truths that cannot always be put into words. How do you describe blue to someone who has never seen it? Could Edvard Munch have written anything that would have expressed terror and anxiety more poignantly than his painting *The Scream*? The language of art is not only helpful when trying to understand what an artist is trying to say, however; art can also teach us about our origins. It can illuminate our study of science and math, improve our grasp of history, add dimension to the creation and understanding of literature and music, and even grant us insights into economics and politics. Conversely, a knowledge of the languages of other disciplines can add immeasurable depth to the study of art. Art does not exist in a vacuum. It is vitally affected by technology, history, philosophy, literature, politics, and so on.

One of the most potentially productive trends in education today is the focus on interdisciplinary studies: teaching math as it applies to science, for example, or relating the various humanities. If we trivialize art and remove it from the core of a mainstream education, we not only deny our students full access to one of humankind's most profound experiences, but we miss countless opportunities to improve their grasp of other subjects as well. Moreover, we deny students access to an extremely useful kind of training and a productive mode of thought. We should also consider that the more legitimately we weave art into the fabric of the general curriculum, the better our students will understand the important role art plays in culture. We not only need valid art programs, but we need to promote respect for diverse approaches within the context of the broader curriculum so students will consider art a potentially productive avenue to explore.

Careers Related to Visual Arts

In the current climate of education, instruction often has to be justified in terms of future earnings potential. Many adults and students alike are unaware of the enormous earning potential of artists, especially those who combine facility in drawing with computer mastery. A common misconception is that students should be guided toward careers with higher income potential and more prestige than those offered in the arts. Yet in our culture, where Disney animators are being paid salaries in the high-six-figure range, starving in a garret is no longer the fate of the successful artist. Some of the markets for such talents include television, video games, movies, advertising, and website design, but there are numerous other areas that can offer satisfying careers and financial security. At a craft fair a few years ago, I happened to strike up a conversation with a man who designed and made jewelry. He mentioned that no one had suggested such an occupation to him until graduate school, yet he not only thoroughly enjoyed his work, but it was supporting three homes and four cars! A former student of mine who is majoring in art showed me a miniature book he had made and explained that there is a definite market for such handcrafted, limited-edition volumes.

> *"A primitive artist is an amateur whose work sells."*
> —Anna Mary "Grandma" Moses

Several careers require expertise in both art and another discipline. Medical illustration; architecture; writing and illustrating children's books; publishing and graphic design; designing costumes, lighting, or sets for plays; photojournalism; and creating aesthetic yet aerodynamic designs for cars and other vehicles are only a few of the possibilities that come to mind. On a recent field trip to a museum of natural history, I was impressed with the terrific artistry involved in presenting the exhibits. What an enjoyable way to combine a love for the arts with the sciences! Art conservation and restoration are two other areas that can blend the sciences and humanities. You would be doing your students a great service by suggesting possible careers that integrate other disciplines with art.

Avocational Benefits of Art

Art can be a wonderful avocation as well, one that can frequently enhance a job in a different area. Another of my former students just received his master's degree in marine biology and serves as a firefighter on weekends. When I visited him at his home recently, he proudly showed me two T-shirts bearing designs he had created. One had been commissioned by his fire department and the other by the aquarium where he worked. Since that visit, more of his work has been commercially produced.

In their civic, professional, and private lives, our students will be presented with problems that require creative solutions. They will need the widest possible variety of approaches to those problems. Music teacher Paula Fair tells a wonderful story of a medical student who detected a heart condition no one else on rounds had caught. When asked how she was able to hear such a slight irregularity, the student replied that she was a trained percussionist. It is not hard to imagine similar benefits for a scientist sensitized to nuances of color, shape, or texture.

In this era of budget cuts, many students may never be exposed to an art class at all. That is unfortunate because even though few of these students will be visual producers, they will all be visual consumers. They will select clothing and furniture, buy posters and paintings, see movies, go to museums, vote on public sculpture, and visit Internet sites. They need tools that will allow them to intelligently interpret and judge what they see. But if students never learn respect for art, and if they never experience the benefits of art training, they will never understand what they have missed.

About *Art Matters*

I teach art in grades one through eight at a private school for academically gifted children. Sycamore School has a formally integrated humanities curriculum in its middle school; but long before then, art is introduced as a subject worthy of study in its own right and is used by most teachers to enrich learning in other areas. In my own classroom, even the first-grade program includes aspects of science, math, music, technology, language arts, history, and social studies. *Art Matters* contains several of the lessons that I have found useful and exciting, plus some that have been adopted or created by teachers of other subjects. Even more importantly, perhaps, it contains suggestions that I hope will inspire you to create your own projects or approaches that are useful in your particular situation. What you will *not* find in this book are the kinds of craft projects in which each student produces a preordained, relatively identical product. Such projects may constitute enjoyable classroom activities, but they should not be confused with a true art experience, which challenges students to make decisions and learn lessons applicable to future projects. I do not consider that incorporating uninventive crafts projects amounts to "integrating art."

I had this broad, integrative, intellectually challenging approach in mind when I was asked to develop the illustrations for this book. I chose an image that speaks as much to the rational, mathematical aspect of art as to its visual realization. It is the geometric representation of the Fibonacci numbers (a geometric series in which each succeeding number represents the sum of the previous two), sometimes referred to as the *golden mean* or the *golden rectangle*. It symbolizes proportions used in structures from the Parthenon of Greece's Golden Age to Le

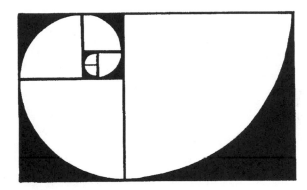

golden rectangle

Corbusier's United Nations Building in New York City. It has applications to Leonardo's famous drawing of the Vitruvian Man, to the composition of such pictures as *The Side Show,* painted by Georges Seurat during the Impressionist period, and to modern Cubist pieces. It has been used in the design of the violin and by such composers as Bartok, Debussy, and Schubert. Some experts argue that Virgil consciously used the Fibonacci numbers to structure his poetry and that other poets of his time did so as well. The spiral inscribed inside reflects the fact that this geometric relationship occurs in nature in certain shells and growth patterns. It seemed to me an ideal symbol for both the intellectual aspect of art and its inherent interconnectedness with other disciplines.

John Ruskin stated that fine art is that in which the hand, the head, and the heart of the artist go together. Perhaps his point is true for achievement in any field. Technical skill in a discipline can be developed wholly within a given class, and people bring their own personal passions to their work. But the intelligence necessary to communicate our achievements to others in meaningful ways requires knowledge of a greater world. Like the diagram of the Fibonacci numbers, education should spiral to encompass endless possibilities.

Who This Book Is For

There are several reasons why you might read *Art Matters*. Perhaps you teach math or science or art and you are looking for ways to improve your curriculum. Perhaps the art program at your school has been cut and you are the classroom teacher responsible for adding so many minutes of "art" to your weekly schedule. Perhaps you are an administrator who knows that students who study the arts do better on such tests as the SAT, and you are looking for ways to add art to the general curriculum without increasing the budget. Or maybe you are studying to be a teacher and are interested in finding new methods to integrate art with a wide range of topics.

This book contains a wide variety of thoughts on how teachers of most subjects can use art to enhance their own curricula, as well as ways in which art teachers can illuminate a range of other subjects. If you are one of the many general teachers who have been told that you must now teach art in addition to your other responsibilities, I urge you to read this book before you panic (and especially before you adopt some mindless cookie-cutter curriculum masquerading as an "art" program). I believe there are valid ways in which even the least artistic among you can give your students useful critical skills and a respect for art that might make all the difference to the next generation of scholars. You will find that the majority of the ideas and projects in this book do not require an unusual degree of artistic ability.

> Art is almost always self-individualizing. That is, given the same visual problem to be solved, a first grader will solve it in one way, a fifth grader in another, and a high school or college student in yet another. I have found that even my first graders can explore some pretty sophisticated concepts.

They can be adapted to a wide variety of ages and abilities. Art is almost always self-individualizing. That is, given the same visual problem to be solved, a first grader will solve it in one way, a fifth grader in another, and a high school or college student in yet another. I have found that even my first graders can explore some pretty sophisticated concepts, and I always try to select projects for my students that I, as an adult, would enjoy doing. I have used many of these ideas with students from grades one through eight, and colleagues have borrowed some of them for their kindergarten or high school students. You know your own pupils best, and only you can decide if a project or concept is too basic or too advanced. I encourage you to consider ways you might adapt the presentation or expectations of each project in this book to make it meaningful for your students.

Organization of the Book

Art Matters is divided into two parts. Part 1 is fairly conceptual and covers what might be termed "thematic" approaches to integration. Although I focus on art integration, you will soon see that these suggestions could be used to integrate virtually all the subjects across the curriculum.

In part 2, I will approach several disciplines separately; namely, social studies, history, language arts, science, math, and performing arts. In each of these chapters, you will find several specific lesson plans designed to integrate that academic content with art. Whatever your area of expertise, I advise you to read through the entire text, because ideas contained in a section for one discipline are frequently applicable to others as well. This is especially important if you are a classroom teacher trying to incorporate a variety of disciplines into a single unit.

Suggestions for Use

One of the primary aims of this book is to encourage teachers to think in new and creative ways about art education. There are a number of ways to use the material in this book. You may incorporate the ideas in your own classroom alone or develop them with a teacher of another discipline. I have tried to

> I have tried to present the lessons in such a way that both the art teacher without science background, for example, or the science teacher without art background can understand and use them easily.

present the lessons in such a way that both the art teacher without science background, for example, or the science teacher without art background can understand and use them easily. Teachers of various subjects might agree to focus on one or more of the concepts discussed in part 1 for a certain time, allowing the students to see the underlying structural and conceptual similarities among all the disciplines.

I firmly believe that any subject is best taught by someone trained in that field, and that every school should have an art specialist. Because I recognize that not every school has an art teacher on the faculty, however, I also offer suggestions that allow non-art teachers not only to integrate art across other academic disciplines, but also to include in their own courses the information or point of view that would have been supplied in a valid art class. Thus a group of teachers could take up the artistic "slack," or a single teacher could integrate art or any other subjects into his or her own class. You will be the best judge of how integration of art could work at your school.

I encourage you to be creative in finding ways to fit the art lessons into your available time frame. Many are very adaptable in length. In several instances, I suggest ways to simplify the project to reduce the time required.

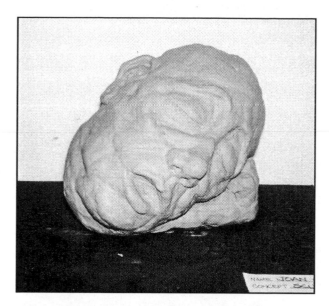

Figure 2. Joan Gabig sculpted this superb piece in eighth grade, while developing her own style.

For many projects, students produce a rough draft or concept drawing before embarking on the final project. This phase could be assigned as homework. In addition, after providing the background and demonstrating the techniques, much of the actual labor of creating the artwork could be assigned as an independent project. If a particular lesson involves use of specialized materials that cannot be taken home, you might consider setting up a work station in a corner of your room or a study hall so students can work on their projects whenever they have free time. The independent project approach also has the advantage that students often can self-select how they complete the assignment (see figure 2). The pupils with artistic talent and inclination can invest much energy in creating the artwork, whereas students with less ability in art can focus their efforts on the academic portion of the project (e.g., an accompanying essay). Both types of students are still learning art principles and concepts and how art relates to other areas of their lives.

Resources for Art Integration

I would certainly urge you to use your colleagues as resources whenever possible. If you are a history teacher who wishes to use appropriate artworks to enhance your study of the medieval period, the art teacher in your building can be a great resource. If, however, you have no art specialist, plenty of books and websites can provide the information you need. There are a wide variety of ways to find out about the artworks and artists you might need to support your curriculum. In the References and Resources at the end of this book, I list every video, book, catalog, filmstrip, or specific website mentioned, and some other references as well. Throughout the text, I suggest resources for specific projects or topics. These are marked with the Fibonacci number symbol so they stand out for ease of location.

Fibonacci number symbol used to denote Suggested Resources.

To find other resources, you first will want to check out your local library or museum, if you have a good one near you. If you browse the library, I would strongly recommend looking in the children's and young adult sections on art. For busy teachers without formal art training, these books tend to be more succinct and accessible than those in the adult art section. Before you even begin looking for visual or historical volumes, however, I would urge you to check out the following resources:

- I strongly recommend that you read *Arts and Ideas* by William Fleming. Fleming places Western art in cultural context. He takes each historical period and presents the arts, philosophy, events, and important ideas of that period in such a way that their interdependence becomes obvious.

- Other books you might want to consider are those that "annotate" the artworks. That is, for each selected painting or sculpture, the author points out virtually every detail from the symbols used, to the names of people pictured, to why the piece is important. I personally love *The Annotated Mona Lisa: A Crash Course in Art History* by Carol Strickland and John Boswell, anything by Sister Wendy Beckett, and *Annotated Art* by Robert Cumming.

- For a succinct and accessible summary of the oft-times baffling art of our own time, *Understanding Modern Art* by Monica Bohm-Duchen and Janet Cook is a wonderful little volume.

- Such books as *Living with Art* by Rita Gilbert and William McCarter and *Varieties of Visual Experience* by Edmund Burke Feldman may be helpful introductions to the teacher who wants an overview of the discipline of art.

- For practical information, *The Art Teacher's Book of Lists* by Helen D. Hume is indispensable.

- Also check out your library's videos, computer CDs, and laser discs. Videos and CDs offer both the student and the teacher enjoyable ways to learn.

A good art museum is another place to find a wide variety of resources. The Indianapolis Museum of Art has a wonderful teacher resource center, which offers rental of slides, videos, and hands-on kits for a nominal fee. (If your museum does not offer such a service, you might suggest that they begin doing so!) If you do not have a museum in your area, you might try contacting the closest one by phone or online to see whether staff there can send you the materials you need. A museum bookstore is also a great place to find such items as visual aids, puzzles, computer software, games, videos, and books.

The Internet is a treasure trove of information and illustrations. Virtually every major museum has its own website, and most computers include some art references in their pre-loaded bookmarks. Some terrific general websites are "Webmuseum," "Artcyclopedia," and "4Art." I would also recommend that you narrow your search considerably if you are looking for something specific. You might, for instance, type "art and math" or "art and science" or the name of a particular artist or work into your search engine. Almost any home page you visit will offer links to other URLs, and it is easy to become overwhelmed if you do not stay focused. On the other hand, you can learn an incredible amount just by browsing.

> S ome terrific general art websites are "Webmuseum," "Artcyclopedia," and "4Art." The Getty Center for Education in the Arts and the National Art Education Association are also great sources of information on virtually any area you might wish to research.

A variety of catalogs will also be of use. Consult the art teacher at your school, if there is one, or ask your school to send for some. I list several at the end of this book, and these companies frequently offer trial periods for videos, so you need not fear wasting limited funds on a purchase that does not meet your expectations.

Finally, the Getty Center for Education in the Arts and the National Art Education Association are great sources of information on virtually any area you might wish to research. Getty offers a wonderful online mailing list server for teachers called "Artsednet." Use the URL I provide in the References and Resources, or simply pop that word into your search engine and it will take you to the site. No matter what your question, someone will be able to answer it or direct you to someone who can.

Suggestions for Handling Nudity in Artworks

The depiction of the undraped figure has been an artistic fact of life since earliest times. It will be difficult, if not impossible, for you to present the works of certain tribal cultures, Classical Greece, or the Renaissance, for example, without encountering nudes. The art history texts in your school library contain nudes, and a visit to a museum or art gallery will certainly include exposure to such pieces. Only you know what approach will work at your school, but here is how I handle the situation.

With young children, I do not explicitly address the subject, although I believe that the earlier students get used to the presence of nudity in art, and take it for granted, the better. Beginning in fourth grade, in the very first class of the year as I am discussing the overview of the course, I explain that during the next few years, we will be encountering several nudes in our studies. I tell my students that if I did not believe they were mature enough to handle such material, I would not present it. I state that artists have always found the human body to be a most fascinating and beautiful subject in all its infinite varieties, and that everyone should treat this wonderful creation with great respect. When they were younger, did their parents laugh at them when they bathed or dressed them? Of course not, because the body is perfectly natural. Some cultures, such as ours, insist on clothing for people above a certain age, and others do not. I explain that I will expect students to behave in a mature way, and that I simply will not tolerate any giggling or juvenile remarks. I have several hundred art books in my room, and as I do not intend to destroy them by removing all the pages with nudes, I need to know that they will be viewed appropriately, just as I must feel I can accompany them on art field trips without being ashamed of their uneducated behavior. If they are embarrassed by a particular visual aid, I totally understand, but they may not choose to express that embarrassment through laughter or any silly behavior. They are welcome to come to me and we will work something out. I add that in all my years of teaching, I have never had a student who was too immature to remain in my class, and that I am quite certain no one in this terrific group will be the first. I repeat this statement at the beginning of fifth, sixth, and seventh grades for the benefit of the new students. After a while the nude becomes so commonplace it ceases to be an issue. ❧

Part One
Concept-Based Integration

"Art is idea. It is not enough to be able to draw, paint and sculpt.
An artist should be able to think."

—Gurdon Woods

There is a general misconception about the nature of visual art. Many believe that the process of making art is simply different in kind from human activities required by such disciplines as science or history or mathematics. I would not dispute that my field has elements that make it separate and unique—some concepts that can be expressed visually simply cannot be communicated verbally. But I would argue that each human pursuit has unique aspects that distinguish it from every other. Mathematicians think in symbols unique to mathematics, musicians "march to the beat of a different drum," if you will excuse the pun. Art education certainly offers alternative approaches to interpreting the world and to self-expression as well. What many people fail to understand is that there are just as many similarities as differences among the arts and sciences. You will find that focusing upon these similarities will help you integrate art far more easily into your curriculum; and by focusing upon them, you can help your students gain more respect for, and understanding of, the nature of art.

There are several ways to incorporate art into other academic disciplines. One approach is to focus upon concepts that are common to a wide variety of disciplines. Understanding that visual artists share many of the same concerns and problems as scientists, musicians, writers, and actors helps demystify the subject and promotes respect and understanding. I recently experienced a wonderful example of this kind of mutual reinforcement, although it happened accidentally.

Each week, I give my eighth graders a quotation, comment, or question to write about. A recent selection was "Form ever follows function," a pronouncement by the architect Louis Sullivan. "You're kidding!" my students responded. "We've been hearing that all year in science!" Sure enough, the science teacher later informed me of her delight when her pupils had come to her with the information that I had given them that quotation. She had been stressing this concept in relation to organs and organisms all year.

In this section, I will discuss a few of many such concepts that you can use to link the disciplines. I will be addressing teachers of a wide variety of ages and subjects, so please forgive me if I sometimes seem to state the obvious. What is common practice for you may be a new and interesting procedure to one of your colleagues. ❧

CHAPTER 1
Concepts and Terminology

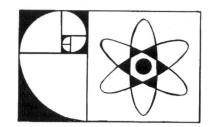

"If everything is art, nothing is art."
—Unknown

In order to present meaningful art lessons to students, it is helpful to familiarize yourself with basic concepts and terminology of art, and to present them to your pupils. Many of these concepts also have related meanings or applications across the curriculum. For example, in art *composition* refers to the way the *elements* of a piece are arranged. In chemistry students may analyze compounds into the *elements* that comprise them. Similarly, criticism is an important feature of literature, music, and so on, while the analytical, critical thinking and interpretation inherent in methods of criticism are applicable to almost any field.

Elements and Principles

Each subject has its own unique elements and principles, concepts that are basic to the understanding and mastery of that particular discipline. The elements I explore and the definitions I use in art class are as follows:

Color: For our purposes, the way light is reflected, absorbed, or refracted by pigmentation. (Even first graders can comprehend this definition if it is presented properly. See "The Physics of Light" lesson on page 116.) Color has three properties:

- **Hue:** The name of the color
- **Value:** The lightness or darkness of the color
- **Intensity:** The brightness or dullness of the color

Form: A three-dimensional, closed figure.

Line: The path of a moving point.

Shape: A two-dimensional, or flat, closed figure.

Space: Some artists add space to this list, defining it as the real or implied three-dimensional area between forms or shapes; that is, illusionary depth.

Texture: The way something feels or the way it appears to feel; its surface quality.

Value: The way the artist uses light or dark in a work of art. Value can be studied as a property of color. Some colors are lighter or darker by nature, or the value of a color can be changed by adding black or white. Black, white, and shades of gray are pure values without color.

Principles: Refer to ways elements are arranged in an artwork. The principles we cover are *balance, emphasis, repetition, similarity* or *relatedness, contrast, overlap, unity, movement, rhythm, distortion, pattern,* and *gradation.*

Balance: Balance refers to the even distribution of visual or physical weight within a work of art. There are several types of balance. *Formal balance* is the placement of like things on either side of a center line, real or imaginary. Figure 3 below is formally balanced, as is *American Gothic,* the famous picture of the farmer and his wife by Grant Wood. (Actually, the picture portrays Wood's dentist and his sister!) Symmetry is the most exact type of formal balance, and some artists use the terms interchangeably. A butterfly is symmetrical, as are all the projects produced in the Symmetry section of chapter 12 (see figures 29–32, pages 137–44). *Informal balance* refers to the balance of unlike things on either side of a center line, as exemplified in the detail of a Huichol yarn painting (see figure 12, page 59). *Radial balance* is the even distribution of weight around a center point as opposed to a center line. A spiral is radially balanced, as are figures 4 and 10 (page 47).

Figure 3. Ashley Gange created this lovely mosaic in the Roman style, producing an illusion of transparent glass with lighter-value tesserae.

Contrast: Contrast simply means *difference*. Artists can contrast color, value, texture, line, shape, or form. Contrast is a great way to create emphasis, and it is also an important principle if the artist wants something to be easily seen. You will notice that in this book, the photographs with the greatest contrast of value are the easiest to decipher. The greater the contrast, the more you notice the contrasted element.

Distortion: Distortion occurs when a subject is altered from the way it is supposed to appear but is still recognizable (figure 5 shows distortion of proportion). Anyone who has ever stood in front of a wavy mirror at a carnival or looked at his or her reflection in a spoon has seen distortion of shape or form.

Emphasis: Artists use emphasis in a work of art to draw the viewer's attention to a particular idea or visual point, analogous to the way a printed word is **bolded** or *italicized*. Emphasis can be achieved through repetition, placement, size, contrast, distortion, or by several other means. In third grade, students focus on emphasis by doing a project featured in *School Arts* magazine several years ago. They trace their hands and feet, then draw in the rest of their body on a much smaller scale. Unlike the rest of the body, the hands and feet are completed in very realistic detail. The distortion of proportion and contrast of styles draw attention to the hands and feet (see figure 5).

Figure 4. In third grade, we create radial designs that would be appropriate for an umbrella. Lauren Thompson created the design for this delightful umbrella as her solution to our radial balance project.

Figure 5. The distortion of proportion and contrast of styles in this work in progress, by Ashley Beuchel, draw attention to the hands and feet.

Gradation: When an artist shows change occurring gradually within an element, such change is called gradation. One example is shading a sphere using subtle changes in value from dark to light. On the other hand, placing black next to white is not gradation.

Movement: Movement is present in a work when the viewer's eye is impelled to roam throughout it. Artists frequently use line to guide the eye in a particular path. The *Mona Lisa* by Leonardo da Vinci displays little or no movement, whereas the outstretched arms of God and Adam in Michelangelo's *Creation of Adam* on the Sistine Chapel ceiling cause one's eye literally to leap across the small gap between the fingers.

Overlap: Overlap simply means placing one shape partially over another. This overlap could be actual, as in a collage (see figure 6), or illusionary, in which shapes or forms appear to be layered. Such a device may help to achieve unity or depth.

Figure 6. Fifth grader Hannah Kennedy created rhythm through repeated and related shapes.

Pattern: Pattern is the regular or random repetition of an element of art with such frequency that the viewer can predict how it will continue. Both the stars and stripes on the American flag form patterns.

Repetition, similarity, and relatedness:
Repetition occurs when an artist uses an element more than once within a work. This device may help unify a piece, create emphasis, or result in a pattern. The repetition in figure 8 (page 40) achieves all these goals. Sometimes the shapes or colors may be similar but not identical as, for example, if an artist were to use various sizes of circles and different ovals in a sculpture as a unifying factor.

Color, line, form, shape, unity, repetition, balance, contrast, similarity, rhythm, symmetry, and distortion are only a few of the terms that have meaning in a broad range of subjects.

Rhythm: Pattern frequently results in the creation of rhythm. The repeated columns on the Parthenon create a regular rhythm. The repeated and related shapes in figure 6 could almost be played like the beats of a drum. Sometimes the rhythm is more undulating, as in van Gogh's brushwork.

Unity: Unity is very hard to define but incredibly important in a work of art. It is the quality of oneness within a work, combined with a sense of completion. Unity may be achieved by the use of a single light source, consistency of style, a unifying theme, and other devices. To explain unity, I ask my students to imagine that I am dressed for a formal ball. I have my hair done, my makeup is perfect, my nails have been polished. I am wearing a beaded gown, fancy jewelry and—high-top sneakers! The contrast will certainly draw everyone's attention to the sneakers (creating emphasis), and because there would seem to be no aesthetic reason for the sneakers, the unity of my appearance would be destroyed.

Integrating Art Principles and Elements across the Curriculum

As you present these concepts, you may find that some of the terms have definitions or applications in your field, which creates a further link among subjects. The study of *pattern*, for example, is common to such disparate fields as math, science, music, economics, poetry, psychology, art, and dance. The teachers in your building might collaborate to create lists of the elements and principles in their fields—such a list might have a lot of uses. In fact, teachers might agree to collaborate across classes or across grades to focus on a specific element or principle simultaneously, elaborating on the similarities and differences in how the term is used across the disciplines. You might agree with your colleagues to divide the year among a series of such terms. *Color, line, form, shape, unity, repetition, balance, contrast, similarity, rhythm, symmetry,* and *distortion* are only a few of the words that have meaning in a broad range of subjects. Students hearing a concept discussed in several classes or different contexts are more likely to comprehend its meaning and nuances. Even within the confines of a single class, you can refer to the various meanings and usages of these terms. I rarely present a new concept or review an old one without citing the word's meaning in a variety of other contexts. Thus, a second-grade discussion of distortion will include references to distorting the truth and distorting sound as well as examples of artistic distortion. My introduction to the concept of elements in grade one will include not only a definition of the word as artists use it, but definitions related to science, music, math, and literature.

Methods of Criticism

The concept of criticism has ramifications in virtually every class a student might attend. Criticism involves judgment, usually by an expert in the medium being judged. The whole concept of teaching "critical thinking skills" implies an attempt to impart not only expertise in a field but strategies for applying that expertise to find the strengths and weaknesses in an argument, philosophy, project, or process. In science, mathematics, sociology, and in fact in every discipline, there are appropriate and inappropriate methodologies. We have all heard of scientific studies that are dismissed because the sample size was too small or the control group was, in fact, not sufficiently controlled. When students enter science fairs, what the judges do is essentially a form of criticism. The scientific method itself is a critical approach that bears a strong resemblance to the basic procedure used in the arts: describe, analyze, interpret, and judge. Historians must employ critical methods when making judgments about a culture based upon newly discovered artifacts or ambiguous remains. How do we choose among conflicting conclusions?

Art criticism offers you a way to reinforce the critical process in your own subject while increasing students' ability to understand art and find connections between art and academic subjects.

The purpose of criticism in art is to form a judgment about a piece. If you decide to discuss a work of art in your class, it is helpful to have a structured method. When I was an undergraduate, the specific method of criticism I learned was the model developed by Dr. Edmund Burke Feldman of the University of Georgia (Feldman 1981). On page 23 you will find a brief outline of this approach, which bears a strong resemblance to the form criticism takes in several other disciplines. You may wish to familiarize yourself with this process or find some other approach that works better for you.

STEPS TO ART CRITICISM

1. Describe

Take a visual inventory of the work by simply listing what you see—a house, a tree, a stream, a woman, or whatever. Keep this process objective. Do not judge or interpret what you see.

2. Analyze

Discuss the formal qualities of the work. Include visual elements such as line, shape, texture, color, value, or form; and principles such as balance, repetition, emphasis, unity, distortion, gradation, movement, rhythm, or contrast. Stay focused only on the elements and principles and their relationship to one another.

3. Interpret

Now you are ready to combine the first two steps in order to discuss your opinion of what the work means. What is the artist trying to say? Is there a message? Is there symbolism? Is there any evocative content at all, or is the work actually about formal issues, such as the relation of one color to another?

4. Judge

Now that you have interpreted what the artist was trying to achieve, do you feel that he or she was successful? Remember, *liking* requires no justification, but *judgment* requires valid criteria. Deciding that a Cubist painting or an African mask is not a successful work of art because it is not realistic is clearly an invalid judgment in light of the fact that physical reality is not generally the aim of Cubists or African maskmakers.

Some models of art criticism include a fifth "funding" stage, wherein factual information about the work is introduced.

Integrating Criticism across the Curriculum

You could simply compare various methodologies. Art criticism offers you a way to reinforce the critical process in your own subject while increasing students' ability to understand art and find connections between art and academic subjects.

Are you a science teacher? In science class, for example, you could do a brief criticism of a work of art using the preceding model, and then ask students how this process resembled and diverged from the scientific method. Too frequently, students are expected simply to follow procedures without truly understanding them, and such an exercise could help them focus on the steps of the scientific method and their rationale.

Are you an English teacher? Literary criticism can follow an approach extremely similar to Feldman's as well. It would be very easy to present examples of art criticism in class, possibly of works in some way related to material the students are reading. ❧

CHAPTER 2
Aesthetics and Philosophy

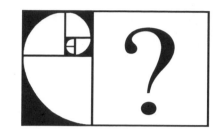

"What garlic is to salad, insanity is to art."
—Augustus Saint-Gaudens

I got this idea several years ago at a conference for art educators sponsored by the Getty Trust. In one of my art rooms, I have a "Big Questions Chart." Whenever a student asks a profound question about the nature of art or artistic production, I add it to the list. Most of art's big questions are aesthetic in nature—that is, they deal primarily with the philosophy of art and beauty.

Here are some aesthetic and philosophical "big questions" about art that appear on my list. You may want to initiate these discussions in your classroom. I suggest you perhaps do some research and develop some ideas of your own before you present the discussion.

What is art? You might ask yourself whether you use the term art *descriptively* or *evaluatively*. If you use *art* as a descriptive term, then any time you or your students create a painting, drawing, sculpture, or whatever, you are doing art. A kindergartner at an easel is "doing art" just as much as Rembrandt did. If you use the word in its evaluative sense, you use the word primarily to refer to great—or at least professional—art. This is the difference between what Daniel Pinkwater, in his book *Fish Whistle,* refers to as "big A Art" and "little A art" (Pinkwater 1989, 171–72). Defining art is really tough. Aestheticians have been trying for years, although the concept wasn't presented as we know it until Napoleonic times. People have a wide variety of answers to this question, but I have a few favorites. In *After the End of Art,* Arthur C. Danto (1997, 30–31) draws from the philosophy of Hegel and concludes art must be "about something" and it must have a "vehicle." Richard Anderson's conclusion in *Calliope's Sisters* that "art is culturally significant meaning, skillfully encoded in an affecting, sensuous medium" is a more precise variation on this theme (Anderson 1990, 238). Dr. Marcia Eaton, in a lecture at a Getty seminar, claimed that art must (among other qualities) "repay sustained attention."

Is there such a thing as an expert opinion? Is everyone's opinion equally valid? Do the views of some art critics or historians carry more weight than others? Is an opinion more valid if the person expressing it has studied the subject at hand, or is opinion just that—opinion?

> *"Beauty obviously depends on the nature of the mind, irrespective of any real quality in the admired object."*
> —Ivan Albright

Can a forgery be art? Before you leap to a conclusion here, consider the following situation. Many years ago, a Chinese nobleman who lived in a province distant from the capital purchased a scroll of great beauty. Its fame spread, and when the emperor heard of it, he ordered the nobleman to give him the scroll as a gift. Unwilling to part with his treasure, the nobleman had an exact copy made and sent it to his ruler. Now, you may be aware that owners of Chinese scrolls add personal comments to the artwork in the form of *colophons*. A colophon may be a poem, a bit of philosophy, a quotation, or an observation, and it is rendered in as beautiful a calligraphic style as the writer can achieve. It is then signed with the red ink seal of the author/owner. Chinese artists leave room for such additions, and these colophons are usually lovely complements to the artwork. They also have the added benefit of providing a very specific *provenance* for the piece. Provenance is the history of the ownership of a work of art, and it can be quite instrumental in determining its authenticity and value. So here we have two scrolls. The original was kept closely guarded and bears the colophons of an obscure albeit noble family. The other—a forgery—bears the colophons of generations of emperors. In this instance, the forgery is far more valuable to a collector. Is it art?

Is it ethical to excavate historical tombs and holy places to expand our knowledge of art history? What about putting artifacts from these sources on display in museums?

Do some cultures value art more than others?

Is one form of art better than another? Sometime over the last few centuries, painting, sculpture, and architecture became the dominant forms of Western art, those considered the most worthy of study. Fabric arts, book arts, and other media have often taken a back seat, a fact that has contributed to the lower prestige of women artists, who frequently have been prominent in these areas, and has influenced our perception of the arts of other cultures. In Japan, brush painting and calligraphy are considered so superior to block prints that a Japanese art history professor whose specialty is the print reportedly does not earn the same respect or salary as one whose area is painting.

What are the connections between political or religious movements and changes in artistic theory?

What makes an artwork good? Should one's aesthetic response to a work constitute a judgment of its quality? Does a piece of art become better or worse as opinions about it change over time?

Integrating Philosophy across the Curriculum

Perhaps each teacher could start a "Big Questions Chart" in his or her room, to help students identify similarities or differences among the considerations for each discipline. Let me warn you in advance, however, that many of these questions will defy easy resolutions. That is the nature of big questions—their purpose is to spur discussion and thought. I would suggest that you begin your chart with a few fundamental inquiries to get the ball rolling. You can easily adapt the preceding questions to a variety of fields. For example:

- What is literature? Is all writing literature? What constitutes science? Is creationism science? What is music? What sources are legitimately historical? For teachers of younger students, this question can reveal your pupils' grasp of the nature of what they are learning. You might have students list every subject they study and "define" what they think it is. (Their answers may surprise you!)

> *"Any art communicates what you're in the mood to receive."*
> —Larry Rivers

- What constitutes an "expert opinion" in science, literary criticism, history, and so on?

- What about examples of forged historical documents? When do they themselves become historically meaningful? What if a scientific study were published under false credentials? Would that negate the results?

- Obviously, archaeologists, anthropologists, and historians, among others, face significant ethical issues about how to conduct excavations. How should society balance religion against the search for knowledge? What do students think about potential uses of mapping DNA? What about cloning?

- Is one branch of math superior to another? Are the social sciences as valid as the physical sciences, even though the scientific method cannot be applied to them in the same way? Is opera better than musical theater?

- In what ways have political and religious thought affected science, literature, music, or the way history is recorded?

- What criteria differentiate good science from bad? Are some works of literature better than others? Is there such a thing as good history? Bad math? ♫

CHAPTER 3
Research

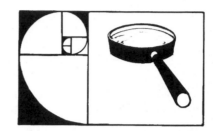

"Are you appreciating the Mona Lisa for the wrong reasons?"
—*New York Times* ad for an art appreciation course

Research is an activity common to virtually all school subjects. It is not unusual to think of research in relation to such projects as history, science, or literature reports, but most people probably do not appreciate the many other forms that research may take or the fact that studio artists do research as well. This research may take a somewhat different form from that used for writing papers, so it could be quite valuable to focus on the various methodologies an artist or art historian might employ.

Realistic photographs: Art teachers usually have some sort of photo file or small library of books or magazines with pictures of landscapes, animals, people, plants, and so on. Even the youngest children can benefit from looking at a photograph of a horse or car or tree when they are trying to draw. I have had students as young as first graders who want to try realistic solutions to visual problems, and many of my pupils are perfectionists who want to draw it "right." Showing them how to create simplified forms and shapes based upon a photograph is far more productive than showing them my personal formula for drawing the subject. Many people make the mistake of assuming that artwork should always be imaginary or "original," yet even the most creative artist usually has a history of practicing from reality.

Visual resources: It is very beneficial to know where to find the type of source you need for a given project. If you want your students to incorporate illustrations of different kinds into their projects, it is helpful to have a small library of books or collection of photographs on hand. Old calendars are a wonderful, inexpensive source of such visuals. So are *National Geographic* magazines. Simply send home a note asking your parents to donate old periodicals, photos, calendars, or books that contain the kind of imagery you require. You might also contact local businesses or your school or public library for books and magazines they are ready to discard.

Library research: One of my projects involves making three-dimensional theater masks (see page 80). Last year, one student chose to do a horse's head and two others created wolves. Fortunately, I have a book that features animal skeletons from a variety of angles, and the illustrations were enormously helpful in designing the armatures for these forms. I also would not hesitate to send a student to the library or to the teacher of another subject for needed materials. Such research is not drastically different in kind from that required by certain science or history projects, but students might not think to associate such resources with the drawing they need to accompany a story in first grade. You can encourage artistic research and attention to detail by having such materials on hand, and I can promise you that such an approach will in no way inhibit creativity.

> All subjects require research, and thus research is a means of integrating art across the curriculum.

Software and Internet resources: Obviously, the computer is another valuable tool for finding such material, whether via software or on the Internet. An art project can be a great motivator for students to practice their technological skills.

Researching an art object: One of the simplest ways to integrate art into another class is to use an art object or project to improve research skills. The history of art offers enormous possibilities for various types of research. I introduce the concept of art history in grade four with a brief unit on the nature of art historical inquiry. I do an exercise that involves various types of research, including oral interview, measurement, observation, and anecdotal evidence (see "The Blue Pot Culture," page 54). If you wish to give your students a sense of what art history or anthropology or archaeology is all about, you might want to do a similar exercise. When discussing research in your class, you might wish to mention that art historians use all these many types of research.

Suggested Resource

If you are not familiar with this approach to the study of artifacts, you might wish to look at a text such as *Art History: A Contextual Inquiry Course* by Virginia L. Fitzpatrick

Independent projects:
Our projects in grades four through seven all require reference to historical artifacts and the culture of a time period or country. I also assign certain independent projects that require students to investigate a specific artist or concept or time period (see figure 7). In middle school, we turn our attention to questions of aesthetics and criticism. Students are asked to write on certain topics and there are opportunities for debate. Such activities may require research via magazine articles, Internet sites,

Figure 7. Seventh graders research twentieth-century artists and present their results in the form of houses made from milk cartons. Shown are "homes" for Andy Warhol, Christo, and Josef Albers.

and other traditional resources, and they all present learning opportunities in a variety of subjects. You will find several examples in part 2.

Integrating Research across the Curriculum

As you can see, all subjects—even studio art—require research, and thus research is a means of integrating art across the curriculum. The methods of art research might suggest some alternative ways to gain information as well as alternative approaches to independent projects in a variety of classes. Perhaps teachers of different disciplines could devise a project that would require several types of research yet result in a single product, such as a well-written science-fiction story based upon some actual scientific fact and accompanied by technically accurate student-drawn illustrations.

At the very least, teachers of all subjects can show how research is used in their own discipline and demonstrate that art requires similar procedures. Here are a few ideas, and I will cover many more in part 2.

Are you a history teacher? Simply assign an artifact from the time or culture under discussion as a topic for research. What is known about the army of soldiers found buried in China? How does the Pueblo pottery of today reflect ancient techniques? How did photojournalism affect policy during the Vietnam War?

Are you an English teacher? When reading eighteenth-century English literature, have your students research the works of William Hogarth. Are your American literature students reading *The Grapes of Wrath*? Have them research the photography of Dorothea Lange or find photographs, paintings, or drawings by Ben Shahn which best relate to the book.

Are you a math teacher? Have students calculate the volume and total weight of the Great Pyramid at Giza. Your students will have to research certain facts before they can figure out the answer.

Are you a science teacher? Your students could research a variety of questions: How did the artists of the Renaissance promote medical knowledge? How do the preservationists at the nearest art museum use science in their work? How did the science of optics affect the work of Georges Seurat?

Are you a Spanish teacher? Have your students research some of the great artists of the culture (or of Indian cultures of Spanish colonial Mexico), pick their favorite, and explain in Spanish why they chose the one they did. ֍

CHAPTER 4
Symbolism

"There are painters who transform the sun into a yellow spot, but there are others who, thanks to their art and intelligence, transform a yellow spot into the sun."

—Pablo Picasso

Of course, no subject employs symbolism more than the visual arts, and in my experience, students love learning to decode such imagery. For children, being able to decode images in art is like understanding a secret language that not everyone knows. For example, on page 110, I discuss *The Arnolfini Marriage,* an extremely famous painting by Jan van Eyck. Painted in 1434 during the Northern Renaissance, it is a tribute to the wealth and power of the rising merchant class, and it is simply oozing with symbolism. Artworks such as this could be used to reinforce understanding of historical times or to illustrate a class in comparative religion. Moreover, symbolism in art is in no way limited to examples from painting, sculpture, fabric arts, or decoration. Buildings offer a rich source of study. A structure may be designed to symbolize the power of the church or state, stability, democracy, victory, or progress. It is no accident, for example, that a great deal of the architecture of our nation's capital reflects that of Classical Greece, site of the world's first democratic form of government.

The important thing to impress on students is that a work of art—from a painting to a TV ad—may have many layers of meaning, and they should look for possible symbols before making any final judgments or interpretations. You could do your students a great service (and help reinforce your own discussion of symbolism) by showing them at least one artwork that has hidden meanings and explaining those meanings thoroughly. Fortunately, there many guides to the symbols in particular pieces of art.

Suggested Resources

To learn more about symbols in various artworks, check out *Annotated Art* by Robert Cumming and other resources listed in the introduction on page 11.

Integrating Symbolism across the Curriculum

Symbolism is a device common to virtually all subjects. In math, symbols range from numbers themselves to the signs for various functions. Symbols in social studies, history, and geography are as diverse as the icons used on a map, the designs on national flags, the American bald eagle, and the Nazi swastika. Psychology is concerned with such questions as the emotional effects of certain images and how the brain processes symbols. Language arts encompasses everything from the letters used in writing to the nature of symbolism itself. In a similar vein, musicians must understand notation systems, including alternative notation systems used by some modern composers, and how certain instruments or motifs are used in compositions to represent animals, happiness, and so on. Scientists work with the entire periodic table, as well as thermometers, weather symbols, solar system imagery, and topographic contour maps, to name only a few. It is hard to imagine a subject without symbols, and interpreting those symbols is frequently essential to understanding what is going on. As you may have learned in English literature, you can miss the entire point of a great deal of poetry if you are unfamiliar with Christian iconography.

It is hard to imagine a subject without symbols, and interpreting those symbols is frequently essential to understanding what is going on.

Television, movies, and advertising are all rich sources for discussions of symbolism relevant to a wide variety of disciplines. Why was Joe Camel chosen to represent that brand of cigarettes and why were those advertisements so controversial? What does the Nike symbol represent, and how do your students think it was developed? Perhaps you could have your students develop a logo that represents themselves, their school, their city, or their state. What do you think about the cowboy in the black hat? What did Darth Vader wear? Then why were the *Star Wars* storm troopers in white? What do we mean by a "knight on a white charger"? What does red represent? What is the "red badge of courage"? How do playwrights and screenplay authors use colors symbolically? What about political parties? Religions? Costume designers?

Symbols can be used in art projects as well. You might ask your students to create symbols for themselves or their family, and to incorporate them into a painting or drawing or sculpture—perhaps a family totem. What about creating a work of art using mathematical symbols or letters as the design elements? What about creating your own alphabet chart? Assign each student a different letter of the alphabet and a specified paper size (fairly small, such as 4" x 4"). Have the student draw the letter and something that starts with the letter—the old "A is for apple" idea. Or have students create the letters out of specific geometric shapes to integrate art, math, and reading. Or link the letter to an author or musician and do something symbolic for the illustration. When all the students have finished, you could simply glue the letters in order on poster board. Perhaps students could study the use of symbolism in advertising or propaganda and create campaigns of their own.

Are you a history teacher? One might spend hours in a history (or social studies or anthropology) class discussing the possible meanings of the obscure designs on cave walls for which we have no verifiable interpretations. Once we reach historic times, of course, we have sources that help us translate glyphs, religious signs, and rock paintings, although there are still images that defy complete understanding. Discussing how the Rosetta Stone was used to decode hieroglyphs, exploring the possible meanings of Aztec picture writing, or showing how Southwest Indian rock writing is similar to the sign language of the culture could offer possible lesson plans to teachers of history, literature, or drama.

Are you an English or foreign language teacher? Perhaps you could compare the writing symbols of various languages. Cyrillic, Chinese, Japanese, Hebrew, Arabic, Sanskrit—many languages have alphabets that can be sources of aesthetic projects. Indeed, Japanese and Chinese calligraphy is a form of art in those respective cultures in a different way from Western approaches to calligraphy. How do various cultures perceive the written word vis-à-vis its artistic properties? How do we treat the written word in modern society? How is this treatment different from the time before the invention of the printing press? Just as music students are frequently asked to create compositions using alternative forms of notation, so too might the creative writing student be asked to tell a story using visual symbols other than letters. Artists do this all the time, although somewhat more succinctly and frequently in an obscure manner.

Suggested Resource

A wonderful video for teachers of history, language arts, drama, Asian studies, and art is *Daimyo,* produced by the National Gallery of Art.

Are you a math teacher? To relate the history of symbols to mathematics, you could discuss how Western mathematics changed after the introduction of the zero and plus and minus signs. You might also decorate your room with posters by artists such as Jasper Johns, who used numbers so colorfully in his work.

Are you a social studies or government teacher? You might use questions such as the following to reinforce points about various types of government and teach about art at the same time: What did buildings in Russia look like under Czarist rule? What style of structure was built under Communism? How did living in the Forbidden City affect the Chinese emperor's relation to his subjects? What did the Forbidden City symbolize? In the Dogon culture of Africa, the roof of the structure where leaders meet to make decisions is kept purposefully low to prevent standing. What does such a design say about Dogon communal society?

> *"Mathematical genius and artistic genius touch one another."*
> —Gosta Mittag-Leffler

Propaganda and Politics in Art

Propaganda is full of stereotypical symbols. Visual symbols help stamp a message indelibly in the viewer's mind. As the old adage says, "A picture is worth a thousand words." A study of propaganda or politics offers some interesting opportunities for interdisciplinary exploration, especially if we use the terms in their broadest sense. To a great extent, the history of art is a history of propaganda. From earliest times, those in control of a culture, whether in the secular or religious realm, have used their patronage of the arts to create monuments to their superiority, wealth, invulnerability, and power. Great examples may be found as early as Ancient Egypt, where tomb art was used to impress the gods with the deceased's worthiness and wall paintings showed members of other cultures as grotesque and unattractive. Mesoamerican and South American pyramids, some of which predate those in Egypt, were used by those in power to stage rituals meant to inspire awe in the populace as much as to impress the gods. In modern times, the use of art as propaganda is often easier to recognize, frequently taking such obvious and unabashed forms as the political cartoon or wartime enlistment poster, and patriotic imagery is as old as patriotism itself. How did we choose the eagle as our national symbol? What if we had gone with the turkey instead?

> To a great extent, the history of art is a history of propaganda.

Integrating a Study of Propaganda across the Curriculum

Television, movie, and advertising images frequently offer subtle kinds of propaganda, and it could be very productive to explore such tactics in an art, psychology, or history class. Another approach to the subject in history, government, or literature classes could involve the concept of censorship. Topical subjects for such a discussion abound, from the photographs of Robert Mapplethorpe to the 1999 dispute between the Brooklyn Museum of Art and New York City Mayor Rudolph Giuliani, in which Giuliani threatened to cut off city funding if the museum did not close its *Sensation* exhibit. What a great lead-in to a discussion of the First Amendment!

Are you a history or social studies teacher? History and social studies classes probably offer the greatest opportunity for an integrated approach using this theme. German artifacts from World War II are rife with distorted stereotypes of blacks, Jews, gays, and other targeted minorities. Our own culture is littered with gross depictions of various targets. Native Americans, Jews, blacks, gays, liberals, conservatives, Japanese, Germans, Communists, and a host of other groups have, at one time or another, been the object of visual calumny. Other, more positive examples still present idealized images of American life or history, sometimes for political reasons. Many socially conscious artists also used propagandistic symbolic imagery to make political statements.

Suggested Resources

Some artists and works that you might want to explore are:
- Pablo Picasso's *Guernica* or Francisco Goya's *The Third of May 1808*
- Many of William Hogarth's series
- The paintings and prints of Honoré Daumier, Théodore Géricault, or Eugène Delacroix, and *The Death of Marat* by Jacques-Louis David
- American painters such as Grant Wood, Thomas Hart Benton, and Ben Shahn will offer some interesting insights into the Depression years and beyond.
- The Socialist Realist art of the Soviet Union is probably the most fertile subject of all, although Mexican Expressionist painters such as David Alfaro Siqueiros, José Clemente Orozco, and Diego Rivera also created a very political body of work influenced by socialism.
- Feminist artists such as Frida Kahlo, Judy Chicago, and Barbara Kruger, to name a very few, offer a different sort of propaganda.

Are you a government teacher? Of course, you can always look at the contemporary political cartoons in your own local newspaper. Most large cities have artists who create in this genre, and a political cartoonist would make a terrific guest speaker in any classroom. A student teacher recently presented a short unit on political cartooning to one of my eighth-grade classes. After a brief introduction to the history of this medium and some fascinating warm-up activities, he assigned students to create their own political cartoons. Whereas his assignment was fairly open-ended, this approach could be a wonderful way to get pupils involved in a local, state, or national election or policy debate.

Are you an English teacher? If we look at nonvisual manifestations of propaganda or political expression, the theme certainly can be used to unify a wider variety of subjects. Do your students read *Animal Farm, 1984, Uncle Tom's Cabin,* or *Gulliver's Travels*? What about the *Bigger Better Butter Wars* or *The Lorax* by Dr. Seuss? Do you discuss the banning of such books as *Huckleberry Finn* or *The Wizard of Oz*?

Are you a science teacher? Do your students learn about Galileo and Copernicus and their conflicts with the church hierarchy of their time? Do they discuss the contemporary debate over creationism versus evolution?

Are you a music teacher? Do students in your classes believe that popular music lyrics contribute to the perceived rise of violence in our country? Do they believe in content ratings on music albums? Do they sing or play patriotic songs? Are they aware that Woody Guthrie's "This Land Is Your Land" had a fifth verse that was not included in the published version because it was perceived as unpatriotic?

Are you a drama teacher? Are there plays that your school drama department has chosen not to present because they are no longer "politically correct"? Drama students might be especially interested in the story behind the play *The Cradle Will Rock*, which was produced during the Depression. When the government, which was funding the project under the WPA, discovered the play's pro-union message, they closed the theater a few hours before the opening. In true "the show must go on" spirit, the cast and audience filed out into the street and over to another venue, and the Mercury Theater, led by John Houseman and Orson Welles, was born. A movie about this event has been released. ◈

CHAPTER 5
Creativity

"There is nothing more difficult for a truly creative painter than to paint a rose, because before he can do so, he must first forget all the roses that were ever painted."

—Henri Matisse

As an art teacher, I have some extremely strong opinions on the way creativity is misused in designing art curricula. Before you present an "art project" to your students, please consider the following. Creativity is a complex concept. It does not always consist of forming something completely original, but rather may involve a new use for an existing item, a new approach to an age-old problem, or simply a degree of mastery that allows the artist to move to a higher level of achievement. Too often, educators seem to feel that "teaching" something about art is somehow "inhibiting" to a child's creativity. Nothing could be farther from the truth. Mastering basic concepts and techniques gives a child the confidence and tools that allow creativity to blossom, whereas simply presenting a blank piece of paper and some new medium or process, no matter how exciting, can frequently be overwhelming. Narrowing the parameters of a project while still requiring each student to produce a unique result can be more conducive to fostering creativity than a seemingly open-ended lesson.

Art Projects That Enhance Creativity

Obviously, my argument presents a challenge to the teacher who has little or no art training, but there are several excellent books and videos that can instruct you and your students in certain techniques (see the References and Resources on page 171). Alternatively, you can simply concentrate on the more conceptual aspects of creativity. There are also projects that focus more on the creativity of the solution than on learning a new skill or concept. Any assignment that forces pupils to stretch their imaginations is a spur to creativity.

I might, for instance, ask my class to do a self-portrait without using any traditional art supplies. In first grade, I pass out scraps of construction paper left over from previous shape projects. Just as we see images in clouds, the students are asked to find an image in their scrap, glue it down, and complete the picture so that other people can tell what it is. In the Social Studies chapter, I describe a lesson called "Create a Culture" (see page 51). I never cease to be impressed by the incredibly creative solutions my students devise for that project. In grade eight, I present a unit in which the pupils are asked to base a project upon a "masterpiece." They must take an accepted work of art and put a new twist on it. This might involve changing the color scheme, turning a painting into a sculpture, or using the work to make a social statement—virtually anything goes. This is a project that lends itself to a computer-generated solution, which may require little or no drawing ability. Over the years, I have been amazed by some of the unique results of this assignment.

Integrating Creativity across the Curriculum

The concept of creativity, its definition, how it is developed and nurtured, and its effects upon culture could be a unifying theme that would naturally include the visual arts. Teachers in each discipline could focus on this concept in different ways. We have an intuitive grasp of what creativity might mean in the arts, but what constitutes creativity in science or math? Is there such a thing as creativity in the discipline of history, or only the effects of creative people on history? (I don't know whether the rewriting of events to omit the achievements of various minorities or women constitutes creativity as such, but it has certainly occurred in art history for hundreds of years!) Perhaps the presentation of research findings in the form of a play might constitute creativity. Perhaps each teacher could make a sign one week and post it where students entering the room will see it. "What is creativity in math?" "What is creativity in science?" "What is creativity in social studies?" Or you might decide to limit the topic to some theme, such as how inventions or a new way of thinking have changed their particular subject.

Lessons that elicit variations on a theme are also conducive to creative thinking (see figure 8). Many art teachers do something similar to the "Reinterpret

Figure 8. Gregory Martens stands next to his project, which incorporates 72 monoprints of a trumpet. He created more than 80 variations of color, value, and style before selecting those he would use.

a Masterpiece" project or require students to produce multiple interpretations of the same image, shape, or form, but such an approach is certainly not limited to art class. A science teacher may, for example, ask students to present a particular leaf in six different ways. The students could focus on the color with chlorophyll or without (the fall color), the texture, the shape, the physical structure, the cell structure, or the veins as lines. They might sculpt the leaf, paint it, draw it, print it, press it between waxed paper, or laminate it. (Given such an opportunity, the students will not only come up with a variety of presentations you never imagined, but they will also learn more about the leaf than they might through simple observation.) A creative writing teacher could present a genre painting and ask students to write three different stories to explain the action. As you read the rest of this text, I hope you will recognize how the projects foster creative thinking. ❧

> Too often, educators seem to feel that "teaching" something about art is somehow "inhibiting" to a child's creativity. Nothing could be farther from the truth. Mastering basic concepts and techniques gives a child the confidence and tools that allow creativity to blossom.

CHAPTER 6
Technology and Invention

"First we shape our buildings, then they shape us."
—Winston Churchill

Technology has had a significant effect on virtually every aspect of culture from the beginning of recorded time. It is another strand that can help weave disparate courses together. Some technological developments, such as the printing press and the camera, have affected a number of different disciplines simultaneously. Indeed, Churchill's quotation might apply to virtually all of humanity's major creations. The history of art encompasses a wide range of technological advances and effects.

Prehistory: The development of the first tools enabled early humans to begin making etchings and carvings. The development of pigments such as ochre in binders such as animal blood or fat allowed vibrant paintings on cave walls. Pottery, the first synthetic, opened the way to a thriving trade in ceramic vessels, and the development of slips, glazes, porcelain, and indeed the wheel itself, furthered this craft. The invention of the loom and the needle ultimately resulted in exquisite tapestries and fabrics.

The Ancient World: Advances in metallurgy, the lost wax process, and new techniques for enameling gave us such treasures as those found in Tutankhamen's tomb or Pre-Columbian Mesoamerica. Technology allowed early civilizations to create monumental structures and sculptures, and the Romans' invention of concrete and their adaptations and improvement to the design of the arch and vault enabled them to reach even greater heights of monumentality and durability.

The Middle Ages: The Moorish use of the pointed arch and the introduction of the flying buttress during the Middle Ages allowed for the soaring majesty of the Gothic cathedrals. An adaptation of the Egyptian invention of the clerestory window filled these cathedrals with light, and the ability to produce colored glass made that light glorious.

The Renaissance: Papermaking on a commercial scale and Gutenberg's invention of movable type had a profound effect upon book arts. The development of oil-based pigments during the Renaissance further changed the face of painting. Renaissance artists also devised a variety of drawing aids—such as Dürer's string perspective grid and Leonardo's camera obscura—to enable them to create uncannily realistic results.

The 1600s to the Present: In architecture, developments such as cast iron, sheet glass, steel construction, reinforced concrete, cantilevering, and the electric elevator have allowed us to build to undreamed-of heights. The modern camera, the science of optics, new cadmium pigments, and the invention of the "collapsible tin" for transporting paints were all factors in the development of Impressionism. Improved means of transportation and communication also had a significant effect on this "modern" art, as did the theories of Freud and Darwin. The movie camera presented artists with an additional tool while raising even greater aesthetic questions, and the introduction of the computer has provided art critics with a virtually endless source of topics for debate. The list is extremely extensive, as most inventions and discoveries that affect society eventually have repercussions on the art that reflects that society.

> Most inventions and discoveries that affect society eventually have repercussions on the art that reflects that society.

Integrating Technology across the Curriculum

In your school, perhaps teachers could present to their students a brief list of the inventions they feel have had the greatest influence on the history of their subjects. Or perhaps your students could be asked to brainstorm such a list. Then, using the preceding summary or one obtained from your own art teacher, you could look for influences that occur on both lists. If a list were created for every subject, you could look for those inventions or discoveries that have been the most universal in their impact. Or perhaps you could narrow the topic to a certain time period, such as the Renaissance, or a certain place, such as China. Maybe you could pick an invention or discovery that has had a profound effect upon your area and trace its influence through other disciplines. However you approach the topic, it can help you weave art almost effortlessly into your own subject. ❧

CHAPTER 7
Affective Education

"Whatever the artist makes is always some kind of self-portrait."

—Marisol

The current rhetoric concerning the moral state of young people has heightened teachers' concern with issues of ethics, tolerance, and general behavior. Our handling of such issues is sometimes referred to as *affective education*. We address problems of cheating, lying, harassment, disrespect, stealing, violence, or bigotry and communicate to students that these behaviors are unacceptable. Beyond that, most of us have rules and messages in our classrooms that inform students before they misbehave that such actions will not be tolerated.

Art classes offer fertile ground for affective education. Subtle and not-so-subtle messages can be woven throughout the study of culture and of art elements and principles. When I present the principle of *distortion,* we talk about what it means to distort the truth. When my students are choosing colors for their bodies in a project on emphasis, I explain that all people have the same skin pigment, melanin. When we study African art, I show a mask with rolls of fat around the neck. This mask leads quite nicely into the topic that different cultures have different standards of beauty. Not everyone believes that waif-thin models are pretty, and only in countries where food is so abundant that it can be wasted is it desirable to look famished.

> You cannot confer self-esteem on students simply by telling them how wonderful they are if they see no personal evidence to support your assertion. True feelings of self-worth come through meeting and overcoming obstacles.

If my students listen carefully, they can learn lessons far beyond facts, theories, and skills. They will really accept that other cultures and individuals have valid outlooks that differ from their own and are worthy of respect.

Figure 9. This haunting sculpture was produced as the culminating activity for a social studies unit on the Holocaust. Leah Pakula used her grandparents' actual numbers on the arms of these ghostly hands. Moral and ethical lessons can be intensified through artistic means.

They will make judgments based upon knowledge rather than ignorance and prejudice. They will find that everyone is different in some way, and that such factors as race, gender, religion, or sexual identity are important only insofar as they expand our insights and enrich our lives. They will develop enough self-confidence to defend personal decisions regardless of peer pressure. They will find powerful yet acceptable ways to express anger or sadness or rebellion (see figure 9). They will learn to value excellence and high standards of achievement. (After all, what do we mean by "raising something to an art"?) They will certainly learn that almost anything is possible if you listen carefully and work hard.

A Word about Self-Esteem

We hear a great deal today about self-esteem, and teachers are taught that one of the most important aspects of affective education is to develop students' feelings of self-worth. I agree, but I think many parents and teachers are laboring under a misconception about how to accomplish this, and this misconception has had an almost disastrous effect on art education. Many people view art class, at least at the elementary level, simply as a therapy/play period, so they feel inclined to praise virtually anything a student produces without regard to true merit, in order to "build self-esteem." Art teachers are frequently advised to refrain from judging student work, on the theory, I suppose, that suggesting something needs improvement might be damaging to the pupil's self-image. I believe this is a deplorable practice on many levels. Imagine this theory being applied to piano lessons or math homework.

In the first place, you cannot confer self-esteem on students simply by telling them how wonderful they are if they see no personal evidence to support your assertion. A pupil who rarely solves a math problem correctly is not going to believe that he or she is terrific at math no matter how many times we say so. We might fairly laud this student's effort and work ethic, but not the product. Of course I believe in general praise that offers the student acceptance as a human worthy of respect, and naturally I do not advocate belittling or denigrating remarks. But true feelings of self-worth come through meeting and overcoming obstacles. Art classes, like any other, need challenging curricula that the students can master if they work hard.

Secondly, young people are not stupid. They know when they are being patronized. "Dumbing-down" the curriculum only denies them skills they will need in later life without boosting self-esteem at all, and simply offering indiscriminate praise is just as bad. If two of my students are trying to draw a horse realistically, and one's work looks like a Kentucky Derby winner whereas the other's resembles a lobster, I am not going to tell the lobster artist how wonderful her drawing is. Not only will my false praise do nothing to help the student achieve her goal of drawing a horse, but it will cause me to lose all credibility with her, and any legitimate praise I may offer later will be meaningless. My job is to help her draw a horse of which she can be justifiably proud. Thus, developing self-esteem is high on my list of affective results achieved through art, but the way I accomplish that end is by presenting challenging projects and teaching my students that they can achieve pretty much anything with proper instruction and hard work. Being able to create beautiful works that are appreciated by both their peers and adults at the school certainly enhances a student's self-image (see figure 10).

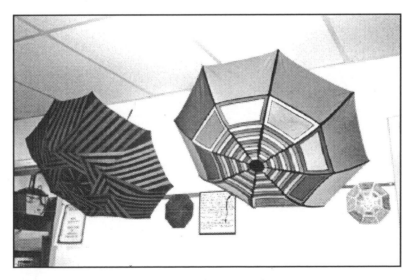

Figure 10. For their project on radial balance, the students design umbrellas. Based on a student vote, two designs are painted on real umbrellas to be auctioned off at a yearly school fundraiser.

Integrating Affective Education across the Curriculum

What is there about your particular subject that furthers the cause of affective education? Does it promote respect for truth? For diversity? Does it foster respect for others? Self-awareness? Intellectual honesty? Perhaps all teachers could post the affective goals for their classes in some spot, so that students could see the common objectives. This would also have the benefit of letting the students know that we value certain affective outcomes. §

What is there about your particular subject that furthers the cause of affective education? Does it promote respect for truth? For diversity? Does it foster respect for others? Self-awareness? Intellectual honesty?

Part Two
A Disciplinary Approach

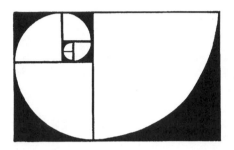

"The sculptor, and the painter also, should be trained in all these liberal arts: grammar, geometry, philosophy, medicine, astronomy, perspective, history, anatomy, theory of design, arithmetic."

—Lorenzo Ghiberti

In this section, you will find suggestions for lessons that target specific subjects. They run the gamut from hands-on art projects to story-telling, the only truly unifying factors being that they reflect an intellectual view of art, integrate art with other subjects, and require higher-order thinking skills. Taken together, they exercise all of Gardner's eight intelligences and require all the operations described in Bloom's taxonomy (Gardner 1983; Bloom 1984). However, they do not represent the type of complete art program that a competent art teacher provides. There is far more to a discipline-based art program than I can cover in this volume.

What I can offer in this limited space is a selection of ideas that I hope will prove both useful and enlightening. That is, they will help you develop ways to integrate art education into your subject and a new attitude about art's place and value in the context of the academic program.

Gardner's Eight Intelligences

Intelligence	Characteristics of Students Strong in This Intelligence
Bodily-Kinesthetic	Keen body awareness. Often can perform a task after seeing it done just once. Physical movement, dancing, making things by hand, and role playing come naturally. Communicate well through body language and physical gesture.
Interpersonal	Learn through person-to-person interaction. Generally have lots of friends, love team activities, and are able to show empathy and understanding. Sensitive to feelings and ideas, skilled at drawing others out, and good at mediation.
Intrapersonal	Self-reflective, self-aware, highly intuitive, good advisors and counselors. Frequently bearers of creative wisdom and insight. Inwardly motivated, with little need for external rewards.
Logical-Mathematical	Tend to think conceptually and abstractly. Able to spot subtle patterns and relationships. Enjoy experimenting, solving puzzles, asking cosmic questions, working with numbers.
Musical-Rhythmic	Very sensitive to musical patterns in the environment: birdsong, rain on the roof, varying traffic patterns. Often can reproduce a melody or rhythm after hearing it only once. May spontaneously sing or compose. May be visibly affected by sounds.
Naturalist	Readily notice patterns in the natural world. Innately sense appropriate categories and are able to group items based on observable characteristics (subtleties in behavior, appearance, texture, sound, smell). May like to collect and study items from nature (rocks, shells, leaves).
Verbal-Linguistic	Able to connect with and influence an audience using the spoken or written word. Enjoy reading and writing, playing word games, making up stories, debating, telling jokes. Tend to be precise in expression, to love learning new words, and to do well on written assignments.
Visual-Spatial	Tend to think in visual images. Often able to discern patterns in shapes, colors, and arrangements of objects. Drawn to visual expression (drawing, painting, designing, working clay). Tasks that require seeing with the mind's eye (visualizing, pretending, imagining, and forming mental images) may be easy and pleasurable.

Adapted from Boggeman, Sally, Tom Hoerr, and Christine Wallace, 1996. *Succeeding with Multiple Intelligences: Teaching through the Personal Intelligences.* St. Louis, Mo.: The New City School, xxviii—xxix.

CHAPTER 8
Social Studies

*"Painting is an attempt to come to terms with life.
There are as many solutions as there are human beings."*

—George Tooker

One of the dominant themes in the study of visual art is that art reflects the culture that creates it. Students often do not realize that different societies value different things, and that those values are reflected in their arts. Although social scientists are aware of the tremendous value of art as a means of transmitting cultural values, this important aspect of art is rarely stressed in the social studies classroom. The activities in this chapter focus on the interplay between art and culture.

Create a Culture

The two versions of this assignment have students describe a hypothetical culture, then create artifacts consistent with that culture. This process may prompt very interesting questions about what constitutes an art object, and these questions are frequently the most instructive part of the process! For example, in museums, we find everything from silver tea sets to mummy cases. Is a modern coffin art? Why or why not?

VERSION 1: SPACE SOUVENIRS
Procedure

1. Begin with a discussion of what constitutes a *culture*, if necessary, then introduce the concept that art reflects the culture that creates it.

2. Give students the following instructions:

   Pretend that you are on a spaceship exploring the galaxy. You land on a planet and discover a native population. On a sheet of paper, describe the culture of the beings you meet. Some things you will want to include are a description of the geography in this area of the planet, what the natives look like, how they dress (if they dress), what they use for sustenance, the level of their technology, what kinds of shelters they live in, their religious or spiritual beliefs, and what kinds of jobs they have.

Version 1: Space Souvenirs

Lesson Summary

Students pretend they have crash-landed on a different planet and discovered a native culture there. They create an artifact supposedly created by that culture (see figure 11, below).

Purpose

To impress students with the vital role culture plays in the development of art forms and the concurrent role the arts play in transmitting culture.

Materials

☐ samples of artifacts from various cultures or of projects created by previous classes to clarify the assignment (optional)

☐ writing materials

☐ variety of art materials and found objects (school-supplied or scouted out by students at home)

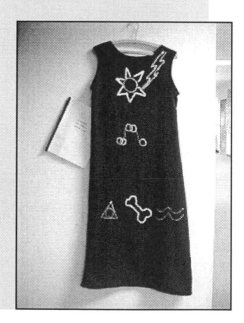

Instructional tip: This portion of the assignment can be as straightforward or as creative as you want. Some students have turned in a detailed diary of their stay on the planet or a ship's log of the adventure. I have even received the singed remnants of a crash-landing! I could easily imagine students working singly or in groups to create a video. Assignments such as this encourage pupils to use their imaginations, enable the less artistically able student to excel, and allow the incorporation of anthropological and archaeological content into the art project.

3. Explain that each student is to bring back a work of art as a "souvenir":

> Create an artifact that would be appropriate to the culture you have described. Think very carefully about this and be consistent. If your natives are very primitive, they might carve a simple sculpture out of wood or collect stones that represent local spirits. If they make portraits, it will be of the local beings—if they have six arms or twelve eyes, so will the portrait. Perhaps you could bring back a landscape of the local terrain, or discover an artifact unique to your culture. It could even be a religious item. Be sure that the item truly reflects the culture you have created.
>
> *Remember: Even though you will make it, this is supposed to be a work of art done by your culture, not your record of the planet or drawing of the inhabitants.* Pretend your work is something of theirs that you have merely brought home with you.

Figure 11. Shea Thompson predicated a civilization in which women were not allowed to speak in public, so they sewed stories about themselves on their dresses in symbols. These symbols were understood by others in their culture.

VERSION 2: BURIED ARTIFACTS

Procedure

1. After a discussion of the nature of *culture,* divide students into small groups. Have the groups move their desks apart or set up screens so that each group can work in secret.

2. Instruct each group to create an imaginary society and write as definitive a description of its culture as possible, without letting other groups overhear. Remind students to consider such factors as geography, clothing (or lack of it), food, shelter, technology, industry, amusements, occupations, and religion (see sample instructions under version 1).

Instructional tip: Social studies teachers may wish to give very specific criteria they want the groups to include. They may even wish to have students model their artifacts upon an actual earth culture.

---

3. Next, have each group create artworks and other artifacts that would have been generated by their culture. They might include frescoes, utensils, tools, books or inscriptions, clothing, ritual objects—the possibilities are limited only by the students' imagination and the availability of supplies. They should definitely consider creating an alphabet or symbol system of some sort. Even the remains of food, such as chicken bones, might be included. Remind students that

   - cultures frequently decorate utilitarian objects, for either aesthetic or ritual purposes.

   - their artifacts should be consistent with the technology of their imaginary culture.

Instructional tip: If the class has been studying archaeology, you may wish to specify certain types of objects for the groups to produce.

Version 2: Buried Artifacts

Lesson Summary

This project is probably familiar to social studies teachers: A group of students creates artifacts from a hypothetical culture, then buries fragments for another group to "excavate."

Purpose

To impress students with the vital role culture plays in the development of art forms and the concurrent role the arts play in transmitting culture.

Materials

- ❑ samples of artifacts from various cultures or of projects created by previous classes to clarify the assignment (optional)

- ❑ screens or dividers so groups can work in secret (optional)

- ❑ writing materials

- ❑ a variety of art materials and found objects (school-supplied or scouted out by students at home)

- ❑ one box or plastic dish tub of sand per group

- ❑ small rakes and toothbrushes for "excavation"

- ❑ glue or tape to reassemble objects

4. After completing their artifacts, students break or tear them into pieces (not too small). Give each group a dishpan or large box of sand and tell them to bury the pieces well. They should bury all the pieces of some objects, and "lose" a few pieces from others.

5. Number each box, then have the groups exchange their boxes.

6. Each group carefully excavates all the items in the box received and tries to piece them together. They then draw hypotheses about the culture represented by these artifacts.

7. Each group pairs up with the group that produced their box, to compare their conclusions with the creators' original intent. This process should prove very revealing regarding the role of art in transmitting culture and the difficulties of re-creating a culture based solely on physical artifacts. For example, piecing together an object will certainly be easier if one finds a fresco showing that object being used.

Instructional tip: There may be faculty or students at your local university or community college who can conduct a "dig" at your school. They (or you) could seed an area with pre-selected objects and lead the entire class in an excavation exercise.

Intrinsic and Extrinsic Qualities of Art Pieces

Social studies, history, or even science or language arts teachers can use an activity such as the following, which is based on close observation of an art object, to reinforce content in their curricular areas. I use the following activity to introduce a multiyear series of units on the art of various world cultures.

 Suggested Resource

See *Art History: A Conceptual Inquiry Course,* by Virginia Fitzpatrick, for further ideas.

THE BLUE POT CULTURE

Procedure

1. Begin by defining *culture* and discussing how art reflects the culture that creates it. The more we know about a culture, the better we will understand and appreciate its artwork, and the longer we study its artwork, the more insights we may gain into the culture.

2. I use a story about a mythical blue pot to illustrate my point. Imagine that while walking in the desert, the class stumbles over a blue pot buried in the sand. Ask, "What can we know about the pot just by looking at it? What can we tell about the culture that created it?"

3. Then discuss the difference between *intrinsic* and *extrinsic* qualities:

Intrinsic qualities are things we can know about an object simply by observing it. These qualities could include size, color, texture, shape, form, location, medium, the artist (if it is signed), the age (if it is dated), the purpose, and so on. From intrinsic factors, we can deduce that the people who made our pot had mastered the art of ceramics and that they had access to blue glaze.

Extrinsic qualities are things we must verify through outside sources. Even intrinsic qualities can offer opportunities for extrinsic research. We might note that the pot is made of clay and that it has a blue glaze (intrinsic qualities), but we might submit the pot to analysis to determine whether these materials are common to the area (extrinsic). We could explore whether the pot was wheel thrown or handmade. Since we found our pot in the desert, we know that one owner of the pot was there on some occasion (intrinsic information). Did he or she live there, visit, or just pass through? (extrinsic information). Imagine that we take our pot to a local museum and find an entire display of similar blue pottery. In reading the notes and talking to the curator, we find that the "Blue Pot People" briefly inhabited the area 500 years ago. We also find that the shape of our pot indicates it was used for ritual purposes. Thus, the artifact has helped us learn more about the people who created it, and knowing more about the culture has told us more about the artifact.

4. Apply these procedures to a real artifact. I use the school building, but you may choose anything that fits your curriculum.

The Blue Pot Culture

Lesson Summary

Trained observation can be a valuable research tool for artists, writers, scientists, historians, and actors, among others. In this activity, students systematically observe the qualities of an artifact, then draw conclusions about it.

Purpose

To introduce the nature of art historical inquiry; to demonstrate the ways in which art assists the study of a society; to illuminate some of the procedures used by archaeologists, anthropologists, and art historians.

Materials

- ❏ artifact for analysis (e.g., use the school building)
- ❏ tools to conduct analysis (e.g., magnifying glasses)
- ❏ yardsticks or measuring tapes

5. Begin by identifying the nature of the artwork and its purpose (in the case of the building, architecture and a school building, respectively). Then discuss the media used to create the artwork. For example:

> We take a walk through the structure to note the construction materials, which students frequently overlook in their daily activities. In the case of other artifacts, identifying the media used might involve chemical analysis or x-rays and could easily lead into research into the science of art conservancy.

6. Discuss what can be deduced about the creator(s) of the artifact and the time period of its creation.

> In our case, the walk yields a clue to the designer of the building in the form of a bronze plaque identifying the group that commissioned the original architect. The plaque records that the structure was initially dedicated in 1959.

7. Size, location, and condition are other intrinsic aspects of the artwork. Have students measure the artwork; in our case we measure the length of one side of the building using an organized yardstick brigade that the students enjoy a great deal. Then discuss location, condition, and any other conclusions students can draw from the artifact itself.

8. Move on to researching extrinsic information through locating blueprints, conducting oral interviews, taking a field trip to a local museum, doing library or Internet research—whatever is appropriate to the artifact you have chosen. For example:

> In the case of a building, a great source of information is the architect's plans. I have the blueprints from my school's first renovation in the mid-1970s. The scale of the blueprints is $\frac{1}{16}$ inch to one foot, so with a little math, we can check the accuracy of our earlier measurements. (In a length of well more than 400 feet, we have come within inches!) Oral interview ascertains that Sycamore School bought the vacant building from the township, and a phone call to the township school corporation headquarters elicits the name of the original architect. One enterprising group visited the township headquarters and viewed the original plans, as well as the publicity for the "new" school. Thus we learned that it was very avant-garde in its day, with movable walls for open classrooms. We discovered that the architectural firm specialized in school design and was responsible for creating schools all over the Midwest. We were able to contact the firm, which was kind enough to fax us a biography of the specific partner in charge of the project.

Instructional tip: You can divide the class into groups and make some of these questions the subject of an informational "scavenger hunt." If appropriate, appoint one student to make phone calls. (The first year I did this lesson, the township secretaries were not thrilled to receive multiple phone calls from my students requesting the same information.)

9. Research the time period in which the artifact was created, and identify how cultural practices and styles of that period influence the nature of the artifact. Draw hypotheses about the artifact and determine how to verify them. For example:

> I have students ask their parents or grandparents about the culture of the late 1950s and early 1960s. We discuss the fact that the original building had no art room or music room and only a very small library, and find that most schools of that era did not have any library at all. I ask questions such as, "What do such facts tell us about education in those years? When were the computer labs added? Is the alarm system original to the building? What does the existence of a school this size say about the demographics of the area? Would this school have existed in this form 50 years earlier? How can we verify our hypotheses?"

Introducing Tribal and Folk Arts

After the introductory Blue Pot lesson, I continue with a general look at tribal and folk arts, incorporating the following points:

- The word *tribal* has different connotations in different parts of the world and in different disciplines. Artists use the word to describe societies that are organized in certain ways, with certain beliefs and a special relationship with nature: Tribal cultures tend to be small in scale and organized around clans or families. They usually have a philosophy that they are one thread in the fabric of the physical and spiritual world rather than being at the top of a hierarchy (the view frequently espoused by technologically advanced groups).

- In discussing tribal societies, whose rituals and beliefs usually involve some form of animism or ancestor worship, I point out that all cultures are descended from people who held such beliefs at one time, and several cultures maintain such convictions today. I repeatedly reinforce one of the affective education themes that permeates the entire curriculum: respect for the beliefs of others.

Instructional tip: Art teachers are frequently presented with terrific opportunities to promote affective education, which I call "life lessons" (see page 45 for more discussion).

FORMAT OF TRIBAL AND FOLK ART UNITS

Each unit begins with as thorough an exploration of the culture in question as time will allow. In lower grades, these explorations revolve around videos, filmstrips, kits, films, and posters, whereas in upper elementary and middle school grades, the presentation involves slides, supported by the occasional video or filmstrip. The unit culminates with a hands-on art project.

Instructional tip: The study of tribal arts offers a wonderful opportunity to integrate language arts as well. I begin each unit by having my students read several short stories, legends, or myths of the culture under discussion.

If you are a classroom teacher focusing on a certain culture or era, you have probably covered several aspects of your topic pretty thoroughly. You might need to present only a couple of filmstrips or videos that concentrate on art. I cannot stress strongly enough the importance of doing this. Simply presenting the following projects without discussion of the society's aesthetic philosophy makes them far less meaningful. The important point to realize is that through exploring a culture, its art will make far more sense. (Perhaps that is why so many of us have trouble with modern art— we do not have enough distance from contemporary society to see the "big picture" yet!) Creating art can help bring a culture to life. The catalogs recommended in the References and Resources (page 175) will offer you a wealth of resources, and I suggest materials I have found useful in each of the lessons (also listed in the References and Resources).

 Suggested Resource

The *Tribal Design* set of filmstrips offered by Crizmac is a good general resource. It offers an overview of the subject and focuses on the individual cultures of Alaska, New Guinea, pre-Columbian Mexico, the Pacific Northwest Coast, and Africa.

PRE-COLUMBIAN STUDIES: HUICHOL YARN PAINTING

The first tribal cultures I explore are the pre-Columbian peoples of Central and South America. For a final project, I considered *molas* (a type of cutwork appliqué) and pottery, among other ideas, before finally settling upon Huichol yarn paintings. The Huichol are a native group indigenous to the mountains of west-central Mexico. They speak a language predating that of the Aztecs and retain many of the beliefs and practices of their pre-Columbian ancestors. They have recently become recognized for their beautiful yarn paintings and beadwork.

The Huichol all create yarn paintings as part of their spiritual journey, and those particular efforts would never be offered for sale. They also make pieces for purely commercial reasons, however, so I do not believe we are violating any religious taboos by creating our own versions. Whereas they use wood and beeswax, we use cardboard and glue. Our yarn is also far thicker, but our results are frequently quite lovely (see figure 12).

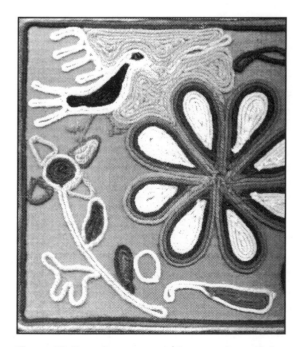

Figure 12. To make a yarn painting, start by outlining each shape with yarn, then spiral inward, as shown in this work in progress. Use strongly contrasting colors.

Pre-Columbian Studies: Huichol Yarn Painting

Lesson Summary

Following a discussion of Huichol culture, students examine Huichol designs and create individual yarn paintings on cardboard.

Purpose

To create a work that looks authentically Huichol; to develop respect for craftsmanship; to explore pre-Columbian culture.

Materials

- ❑ books and resources showing yarn paintings, to give students ideas
- ❑ manila paper
- ❑ pencils
- ❑ knitting yarn in various colors
- ❑ quick-drying, clear glue such as Aileen's Tacky Glue (The stickier the glue, the better.)
- ❑ cardboard in 7" x 10" rectangles and 10" diameter circles
- ❑ sharp scissors
- ❑ pushpins (optional)

Suggested Resources

I have found the video *The Art of Mexico, Central America, and South America* by Lucy Davidson Rosenfeld to be very informative for an overview of tribal cultures of the Americas.

Some sources you might use to discover more about the Huichol are:

- *Huichol Indian Sacred Rituals,* by Mariano and Susana Valadez [book]
- *Art of the Huichol Indians,* edited by Kathleen Berrin [book]
- *Cuentos de las Fibras: Stories of the Yarns* [filmstrip], which includes a demonstration
- *Touching the Timeless* [video]. The first half of this video records the Huichol pilgrimage to hunt the sacred peyote; I use it to make some affective points about drugs.
- Ethnic Arts and Facts offers a wonderful kit, *Huichol Indians of Mexico: A Culture Kit,* containing among other resources a small yarn painting. I recently purchased a second piece at the Field Muscum storc in Chicago, and I would guess other museums might offer them as well.
- You can also see beautiful examples by typing "Huichol" into your Internet search engine.

Procedure

1. Begin by exploring the culture, especially the symbols and legends used by the Huichol and their methods and reasons for creating yarn paintings.

2. Explain that students will be creating their own authentic-looking yarn paintings. Discuss the types of images that appear in the yarn paintings and those that do not. (For example, racecars and polar bears are obviously inappropriate images.) Some students like to make up a myth or legend and then "illustrate" it, which is a lovely way to proceed. It also offers further possibilities for curriculum integration.

3. Give a demonstration of the techniques and processes students will be using, so they become aware of technical difficulties.

4. Have each student create a rough draft of his or her intended project on manila paper. Place a few pieces of round and rectangular cardboard on each table. Allow students to choose their desired shape and trace around it on the manila paper, so they can draw their sketch to scale. (This helps students recognize size constraints.)

Instructional tip: You can control the time required for this project by adjusting the size of the cardboard. I give my students several weeks to work on their projects in class, but you could choose a much smaller size for a shorter-term project.

5. Review and approve each student's sketch for cultural appropriateness of the images and technical difficulties. Many students have to be reminded of the limitations of working with yarn and glue. I frequently encourage my students to simplify their designs. One or two large images rendered well are better than tiny drawings that are frustrating to achieve with the designated materials.

6. Give each student a piece of cardboard. (If the cardboard is decorated in some way, be sure students use the plain brown side.) Have students copy their drafts onto the cardboard in pencil.

7. The students begin by placing a thin border of glue at the extreme limits of the cardboard and making a border at least three strands wide around the edge of the piece. They then squeeze a small bead of glue along each pencil line of their drawing, outlining every figure on the cardboard. They can use pushpins as needed to hold the yarn in place on the outlines until the glue dries.

8. After allowing the yarn outlines to dry completely (which makes filling in the images much easier), students fill each figure, starting at the outline and spiraling inward. The background is treated in the same fashion: by sectioning off large areas and treating them as positive shapes.

9. One of the lessons I want to convey with this project is respect for the exquisite craftsmanship inherent in such works. I do not accept any slipshod or careless projects. No cardboard should show when the project is complete, so I caution the students to hold their pieces up to eye level frequently and look directly at them. Working at an angle, perspective can cause the illusion of tight work when there are actually gaps.

Note: After the creation of the initial design, this project may seem to be a purely hands-on craft, and I would agree that it is more purely tactile than most. However, I believe it is valuable on several levels. Many jobs in life require simple hard work and perseverance once the original idea is conceived, and I believe good craftsmanship should be a goal in all our endeavors. But more importantly, projects like this are really visual research papers. They show whether the student has some sort of feel for the culture under discussion, and help reinforce the values of the society or era being studied. And since you will stress good composition and strong contrast of color and value, students have many visual decisions to make.

African Tribal Arts: Mask Drawings

Lesson Summary

Students create two-dimensional interpretations of three-dimensional African masks and carvings. This is a good project for a teacher who does not feel adept at drawing. Your main job will be to insure that the student produces something powerful and authentic, rather than a Western-style clown or smiley face.

Purpose

To discuss different cultures' views of art and beauty, as well as questions of utility, spirituality, and artistic influence (consult the suggested resources for information); to force students to consider negative space (background) in a way a sculptor does not; to understand concepts such as abstraction, simplification, distortion, and emphasis; to explore composition and solutions for negative spaces that will enhance rather than detract from or overpower the subject.

Materials

- plastic drop cloths for tables
- painting smocks or old adult-size shirts turned back-to-front
- plastic knives
- manila paper
- discardable containers
- color reproductions and photocopies of masks to use for ideas
- 12" x 18" and 18" x 24" sheets of construction paper (preferably black or primary colors)
- oil-based livestock markers or similar material (oil paint in stick form)
- oil-cutting cleanser such as Goop or GoJo
- raffia or small shells (optional)

AFRICAN TRIBAL ARTS: MASK DRAWINGS

The second unit I teach covers African art and its influence on the work of black artists in America and on twentieth-century art in general. After a strong focus on African masks and sculpture, I present the following lesson in which students draw a mask or carving using oil-based markers. You could easily do other projects based upon textile design, dolls, jewelry, or carving.

Suggested Resources

- I strongly recommend the following videos: *African Art and Culture, The Art of the Dogon, African American Art: Past and Present* [the last is a three-part series.]
- Ladislas Segy's book, *Masks of Black Africa*, is also quite helpful.
- A nice source of inexpensive ideas is Irene Tejada's *Brown Bag Ideas from Many Cultures*.

Materials tips

- This project is messy! Be sure to cover work areas and students' clothing.
- At our local farm bureau co-op, I can buy a box of twelve large sticks of oil-based livestock markers in assorted colors for about twelve dollars and a dozen of a single color for only slightly more. (These prices may range greatly depending on your location.) A similar material is sold in art supply stores, but there a single medium-sized stick may cost six or seven dollars.
- With young children, I would substitute oil pastels, crayons or colored chalk, or even markers for the oil-paint sticks. If using crayons or markers, use white or light-colored paper.

Procedure

1. It is a good idea to experiment with this very versatile material before offering it to your students. To use it, merely draw as you would with any material. Apply the "paint" heavily.

2. Set up work areas so that each student has access to oil sticks, a knife, and a container, and has adequate space to work. The most economical arrangement allows several students to share. I have my room arranged so that six students can share three containers, one box of paint sticks, and several knives. I also provide manila paper at each table on which to clean paint sticks.

3. Students must begin by peeling the dried "skin" off the oil sticks using a plastic knife. Caution them to scrape, not cut chunks. You do not want the peelings falling on the floor or even on the tables too much, so make sure they hold the stick over a discardable container.

Figure 13. These African mask projects were made by fourth graders.

Instructional tip: I have had students use the discarded peelings in their projects by pressing the wet side onto the surface of their work.

---

4. Some students create original drawings from their impressions of the introductory material (see figure 13). For those who prefer to draw from models, provide a large array of visual aids, both good color reproductions of masks and some simple copies that the pupils can take to their seats and get dirty.

5. Demonstrate techniques for drawing with the paint sticks: While wet, the colors mix very well. This will allow far more variety—since the palette is somewhat limited—as well as helping to reinforce color theory. The paint dries overnight, and once it is dry, you can simply draw over anything you want to change. You can also layer two contrasting colors and scrape through the top coat for textural effects.

6. Give students construction paper and allow them to begin their masks. You may wish to have them experiment with 12″ x 18″ paper, then when they are comfortable, do a final project on an 18″ x 24″ sheet. You may also encourage students to enhance the final works with raffia or small shells.

7. At the end of each period, simply stack the wet pieces for storage. You can easily "unpeel" them to work on again another day.

Native American Art: Pottery Making

Lesson Summary

Students create pottery using a procedure that mimics ancient Pueblo techniques but is simplified because of the limited time frame of a school project (see figure 14). To simplify the project even further, you could choose to make a small pinch pot, although I prefer a more authentic process.

Purpose

To teach appreciation for the ancient craft of pottery and the techniques of early potters; to emphasize the Native Americans' relationship with the earth.

Materials

For 40 students:
- ☐ 50 lbs. self-hardening clay
- ☐ 40 12" x 12" zipper storage plastic bags
- ☐ 41 disposable plastic soup bowls (in the paper goods section)
- ☐ 1 cheap plastic tablecloth
- ☐ 41 sheets of manila paper
- ☐ pencils
- ☐ scissors
- ☐ water
- ☐ margarine tubs or similar containers for water
- ☐ 1 old sheet or drop cloth per work area
- ☐ 2–3 small sponges and craft sticks (or pottery tools) per work area
- ☐ visual materials for researching decorative motifs
- ☐ acrylic or tempera paints
- ☐ small paintbrushes

NATIVE AMERICAN ART: POTTERY MAKING

The culminating activity of my series of units on tribal art is to create a pot using (fairly) authentic techniques. Once again, you might choose to culminate a unit on Native Americans with a wide variety of possible activities. You might assign different groups to research various nations and create appropriate artworks. Or you might choose weaving, sandpainting, beadwork, leatherwork, woodwork, or the creation of totems.

Suggested Resources

- The best preparation for this project is to view *Daughters of the Anasazi,* a video featuring the famous Acoma potters Lucy Lewis and her daughters demonstrating traditional methods.
- I also recommend the videos *Sacred Ground: The Story of the American Indian and His Relationship to the Land* and the second half of *Touching the Timeless.*

Materials tips

- I use self-hardening clay for the pots because sometimes clay explodes during kiln firing, and I choose not to deal with this problem. I buy a very inexpensive clay from Triarco, but other brands also work quite well.
- Acrylic paints are preferable for decorating the pots, because tempera has a greater tendency to flake. Because I stress authenticity, I limit colors to black, white, terra cotta, brick red, and the gray of the clay itself.

Procedure

1. Each pot will be formed in a plastic bowl. It is important to line the bowls so that the pots can slide in and out easily. I make plastic liners that will last for years (I do not recommend newspaper) using the following procedure:
   - Cut the rim off one plastic bowl, make a straight slit down the side, and carefully cut out the bottom.

- Flatten out the strip that was the side of the bowl and trace around it onto a piece of paper. Trace around the bottom piece as well.

- Cut out the tracings and make sure they fit into the sides and bottom of an intact plastic bowl. If they fit, then copy the tracings on the plastic tablecloth.

Figure 14. Pots based upon Native American styles form an impressive display.

- Fold the tablecloth several times before cutting so you can cut several liners at once.

2. Practice the pot-making procedure in advance so you can demonstrate it to students proficiently.

3. Place a ball of clay about the size of two fists into each plastic zipper bag. Cover students' work surfaces and place containers of water and some tools at each station.

4. Give each student a bag of clay, a plastic bowl, and a set of liners. Have the students write their names on their plastic bags. Then demonstrate the pot-making procedure:

5. Divide the clay ball roughly in half, placing one half back in the bag and making a ball from the other.

6. Flatten the ball into a pancake about $3/8''$ thick. Place the pancake in the cupped palm of one hand and press gently with the fingers of the other hand to create a shallow bowl.

7. Center this concave form inside the lined plastic bowl and press gently but firmly until the clay conforms to the form of the bowl. Make sure the edges of the clay do not become too thin. Smooth the interior.

8. Depending on the size of the original ball, the clay might not reach to the top of the bowl. To increase the height of the pot, add coils as follows:

- Take the ball of clay from the bag and roll it gently but firmly on a hard surface until it creates a "snake" longer than the circumference of the pot and thicker than the top rim of the clay pot.

- Lightly score both the rim of the pot and one side of the coil with a stick or tool. Dip your fingers in water and run them over the scored edges.

- Arrange the coil on the rim, scored edges together, and work the pieces together until any ridges disappear.

9. Continue this process until the pot reaches the top of the plastic bowl, removing it from the bowl whenever necessary to smooth the outside surface. Always return the pot to the plastic bowl so it does not lose its form, and make sure the liner is in place.

10. Students may choose to stop at this point or continue to build their bowls into pots. If they decide to continue, remind them that they may build *up* or *inward* but not *out*. Early pots were formed in the image of gourds, so advise students to keep the general contours simple and as symmetrical as possible. They also should make sure the clay does not rest on the rim of the plastic bowl, and should keep the walls of the pot as even as possible, to avoid cracking during the drying period.

Instructional tip: This process will probably take more than one period. (Elementary-age children may need four or five classes to form the pot, but older students can finish far more quickly.) When not working on their pots, students should store them in the plastic bags. Be sure they add just a little water to the clay before sealing the bag *tightly.*

---

11. When students are satisfied with their pots, have them carve their names carefully on the bottom and set them out to dry.

12. After researching appropriate motifs, the students should sketch out their ideas for decorating their pots on manila paper. Approve the designs.

13. Students sketch their designs lightly on the dried clay in pencil, then paint them.

Instructional tip: Never paint "wet next to wet." Always let an area of paint set up before painting any areas that touch it.

Oriental Art

Chinese and Japanese art and history offer rich opportunities for exploration. I chose *sumi-e,* or black ink painting, as a final project, but these societies have such rich cultures that you have a vast array of activities to choose from: kites, origami, working with clay, woodcuts or other type of printmaking, embroidery, sculpture, lacquerware, carving *chops* (red ink seals)—the list is lengthy.

Suggested Resources

- *Chinese Art and Architecture* [two-video set]
- *Chinese Painting* and *Art of Japan* [filmstrips]
- *Daimyo* [video]

CHINESE AND JAPANESE BRUSH PAINTING

Figure 15. These *sumi-e* paintings are almost completed.

One reason I chose brush painting is that it often looks very simple but is, in fact, *extremely* difficult. Normally I am very careful to pick projects that are challenging but yield a large measure of success to anyone willing to work hard. This lesson is an exception. Although most of the students ultimately will be satisfied with their products, and the average person who sees them in the hall will be impressed, they almost never will pass scrutiny by an informed eye (see figure 15). *Sumi-e* masters study for decades to perfect their techniques. There is a wonderful story of an artist who visited a tiger in a zoo for one solid year without making a mark of any kind. At the end of the year, he pulled out his brush and, with a few deft strokes, perfectly captured the animal's form and spirit. Thus the Chinese proverb: "First become the tiger—then paint the tiger!" *Sumi-e* conveys a wonderful lesson, especially to gifted students for whom many things come very easily and quickly. Not everything that *appears* simple *is* simple.

Authentic Chinese or Japanese brush painting requires years of experience and is difficult to achieve even for an art teacher. Therefore, if you select this project to culminate a unit on Eastern studies, you might choose one of the following options:

- In Indianapolis we have an organization called Young Audiences that provides experts in visual and performing arts for school programs. You might locate an artist skilled in *sumi-e* techniques through a similar group in your town or city.

- If there is no such organization in your area, you might check with your local chamber of commerce to see whether there are Chinese or Japanese cultural organizations in your area that would put you in touch with such an individual.

- Depending on the diversity of your student body, there might be a parent or other relative who could demonstrate this art or lead a class project.

- Finally, you might simply provide examples of brush painting, some black tempera watered down to an inky consistency, bamboo brushes, and newsprint, and let the students copy existing brush paintings. Copying masterworks is an appropriate technique in this case. In the history of Chinese art, copying was considered not only instructional but a sign of respect for the original work. ❧

> *"A good art program is an essential part of a school curriculum. From my art classes, I have learned many things, such as how to look at the world from different perspectives and unique ways to express myself."*
> —Ashley, Sycamore student

CHAPTER 9
History

"Art among a religious race produces relics; among a military one, trophies; among a commercial one, articles of trade."

—Henri Fuseli

Perhaps the easiest subject to integrate with art is history. Certainly, art taught in a historical and cultural context makes more sense and is more enlightening than art considered separately, and a history teacher who illustrates each unit with appropriate art from the period can only improve the students' grasp of and connection with the time or culture under discussion. Most art history books follow a time-line approach, so one need simply turn to the era under discussion to be presented with a wealth of possible visual aids.

In an ideal world, every school would have a highly trained art specialist who could teach art history in depth and offer strong support to the history faculty at the same time. *Art Matters* offers several suggestions for those of you who teach in such a situation. For those of you who would like to incorporate art history but do not have the services of an art specialist in your school, the following pages present a very brief summary of the concepts and projects I cover in my classes.

Please forgive my oversimplification of the philosophical aspects. I cannot go into detail in a volume such as this, but the outline of historical background should help you present the art in context. Although some of these projects require drawing skills, you will find that you can still adapt them even if you are not confident of your drawing ability. Perhaps these ideas will even allow you to discover a hitherto hidden drawing talent.

Discipline-based art history education can be approached in several ways. In the Getty model each art unit covers four topics: production, history, criticism, and aesthetics. Such an approach is useful if you will have the same students for only one year. In contrast, the program I have evolved over the years does not give equal attention to these considerations simultaneously. My first, second, and third graders focus on elements and principles of art. I use famous works as visual aids but do not stress their historical or cultural contexts. In grades four through seven, the emphasis is entirely on such factors. (Production and questions of aesthetics and criticism are always present.)

Suggested Resources

Art history volumes are readily available at libraries, museums, and bookstores. The Internet is another fertile source of such material. I will include only a *very* few suggestions for each period, since you can so readily find examples on your own.

An Integrated Approach to Art History

In middle school (at Sycamore, grades 5–8), we have designed what I believe to be a unique approach to integrating art with academic subjects. All humanities courses are organized around a historical time line. Fifth graders begin with prehistoric times and move through the medieval period. Sixth graders start with the Renaissance and proceed into the latter part of the nineteenth century, and seventh graders finish that century and explore the twentieth. Thus, a student in grade five who is studying Greek and Roman art in my class is simultaneously learning about Greek and Roman history and reading the myths and legends of those cultures in other courses. This approach sometimes extends beyond the humanities to include science and technology as well.

There are myriad advantages to this type of interdisciplinary approach, to both the student and the teacher. Once the time line is in place, teachers do not need to spend hours in meetings, creating or coordinating themes and other linking devices. (Themes flow quite naturally from a historical approach, so teachers who enjoy a thematic perspective can still use that format.) Field trips serve everyone, so money and time are more efficiently allocated. Teachers can focus on those aspects of a culture that reflect their areas of expertise, knowing that other facets will be covered extensively in other classes. When those aspects do overlap—for instance, when I discuss a literary work or historical event in art class—I am either filling a gap or, more likely, reinforcing material presented in other classes.

For students, this arrangement makes much more sense than a scatter-shot approach. They can immerse themselves in a period, experiencing it from a wide range of viewpoints and hearing underlying truths reinforced by a variety of teachers. They do not need to change mental gears every class period. They begin to see cause and effect, the ebb and flow of historical change.

I have several reasons for preferring the time-line idea over a straight thematic approach. I have always taught art history sequentially. One of my main goals is to have students understand why the art of a certain time or place looks the way it does, and much of that understanding relies on a knowledge of what came before. Learning that the Renaissance involved a rebirth of certain Classical philosophies is rather pointless if you have never studied Classical thought. Being told that the Impressionists were creating a type of art that was highly different from the academic work so popular at the time has little impact if you are totally unfamiliar with the products of mainstream painters and sculptors. And why did the Impressionists choose just that time to break away? Why did this movement not emerge in the Middle Ages? It is a lot easier to discuss the profound effect of African masks and sculpture on twentieth-century art if you have already explored such pieces in depth. Discussing artists and movements out of chronological order requires constant backtracking, and such an approach rarely allows the student to see the big picture. The same is true for the study of history in general. A sequential, integrated humanities approach allows each subject to retain its discrete nature. It is an idea you might want to explore at your school.

Prehistory

The two predominant art forms of prehistoric times are cave painting and pottery. Cave painting was more common to Paleolithic times, whereas pottery—the world's first synthetic—became practical only after human-kind had ceased its nomadic wanderings and formed settled communities in the Neolithic era. For many years, I used the Native American pottery-making project (page 64) as the culminating activity for a unit on prehistoric art. I simply showed a more universal array of pots, from the earliest examples found in China, to those from the Mediterranean region, to examples from the Americas. I focused on the qualities these examples shared— abstract designs, especially spirals, wavy lines, zigzag lines, circles, and dots; repetition; rhythm; movement; pattern; form, especially gourd and animal contours; and a restricted color palette. It really is amazing that cultures oceans apart have produced such similar themes and images throughout their histories. These parallels among cultures would in themselves be a wonderful topic for a history teacher to explore.

Of course, there are many other potential prehistoric art projects:

Handprints: Students could create handprints, as some early people did, either by dipping their hands into a red liquid such as tempera paint or by blowing powdered paint around one hand with a straw.

Rock carvings: They could draw or carve into real rock or dried mud or clay.

Chalk drawings: They could draw with sidewalk chalk on a sidewalk or a stone or brick wall.

Jewelry making: They could make jewelry with found materials, especially if they live in an area where feathers, small bones or shells are easy to find.

Cave Paintings

Lesson Summary

The class creates one large cave painting or individual students create their own, using kraft paper and charcoal.

Variation: Students make cave paintings using images that members of modern society might choose

Purpose

To reinforce the concept that art contains culturally significant content; to show that great art has existed from earliest times; to illuminate the life of early humans; to demonstrate that realism *and* abstraction both have prehistoric beginnings.

Materials

- ❑ examples of cave paintings as visual aids
- ❑ scissors
- ❑ brown kraft paper in rolls or paper grocery bags
- ❑ vine charcoal (preferred) or black crayons
- ❑ hairspray or acrylic spray

CAVE PAINTINGS

An alternative to pottery, particularly for young children, would be faux cave painting. After studying the lifestyle of early communities and their dependence upon the animals they hunted for their food, clothing, shelter, implements, and so forth, and after viewing several examples of cave art, the students could discuss what sort of imagery appears on cave walls and why the artists might have chosen those subjects. It is important to note that both naturalistic and abstract images have existed since earliest times.

 Suggested Resources

The caves of Altamira, Spain, and Lascaux, France, are exceptionally rich sources for visual aids, and caves in northern and southern Africa and Aboriginal rock paintings from Australia are equally fascinating.

Materials tips

- Note the spelling of kraft paper, with a *k,* if you are looking for it in a catalog.
- If you use grocery bags, cut down one side seam and carefully cut along all the bottom edges to remove the bottom of the bag. Spread the paper open to lie flat, and if it is decorated, use the plain side. For larger projects, tape or staple several bags together from the back.

Procedure

1. Display plenty of visual aids of cave paintings for students' reference.

2. Crumple the paper to form a textured surface analogous to the rocky interior of a cave wall. Depending on your circumstances, you could spread the crumpled paper on the floor, tack a great deal of the paper on a large wall, or line a convenient storage closet or small room. Doing so allows the class to work together to create one large project.

Alternatively, students could work individually at their desks on single sheets of paper.

3. If you can do this project in an environment with minimal light, so much the better. Raking light is best; that is, light that strikes across a surface from the side. Perhaps you could pull down all your shades but one or darken the room and use a single, unshielded bulb. Flickering light that simulates torchlight would be ideal.

4. Encourage students to look for creases in the paper that suggest parts of an animal or design before they begin drawing, and to incorporate these into their drawing. Then simply have the students draw animals and abstract designs on the crumpled paper, imitating the style of cave paintings.

5. If charcoal is used, you may wish to spray the finished work with hairspray or acrylic spray as a fixative to prevent it from smearing.

Variation

For a somewhat different slant on this lesson, you might discuss what subjects our earliest ancestors drew on their primitive "canvases" and why. Then you might encourage your students to draw the images that they feel a member of contemporary society might inscribe. Ask questions such as the following to guide students' thinking: "What is vital to our well-being?" "What aspects of our environment might we want to have power over?" "What would we hesitate to draw?" "What would we render in symbols?"

Ancient Egypt

We follow the development of Egyptian society from its early years until Roman times, and we discuss some of the controversies that have arisen recently about the nature of these early people. I am sure that any history teacher reading this book has personal opinions about such issues, but there is one area of disagreement which is predominantly artistic in nature that I would like to address. It goes to the heart of the premise that art reflects the culture that creates it.

When I was an undergraduate, my art history teachers taught me that the reason large stone statues from Egypt were so rigid and blocklike was that Egyptian sculptors, working in extremely hard materials, never figured out how to make arms and legs stick out from the bodies the way later Greeks did. Personally, I find it hard to believe that a society that could build the pyramids and perform brain surgery could not figure out a way to drill through hard stone if they had wanted to. Certainly, after the Greeks conquered Egypt, we would have seen a drastic change in artistic style if the only reason for the earlier look had been technological limitations.

Moreover, the Egyptians were not isolated; they had a great deal of interaction with other Mediterranean cultures and could have brought such technology home had they so desired.

A wonderful exhibit at the Indianapolis Museum of Art offered a different and, in my opinion, superior interpretation of this stylistic choice. The creators of the exhibition suggested that because the purpose of most of these figures was to house the soul, or *ka,* in the event that the embalmed body was rendered unfit for this task, it was vital that the figure endure intact for eternity. Even a cursory examination of Greek sculpture will show that very little of it has survived without losing essential body parts. Would you like your soul to exist eternally minus an arm or a leg? Even those statues that were not intended for this purpose were still meant to last forever. Keeping the various appendages as unified with the body as possible created stability and reduced the likelihood of unfortunate accidents.

Debates such as this demonstrate clearly why it is so necessary to explore a culture thoroughly before commenting on the art or other products of the society. Presenting such issues to your students is a wonderful way to inspire research, increase respect for the work of art historians, and encourage creative thinking. Another good topic for such debate is whether we have the right to dig into old tombs in the interests of science, history, sociology, or education in general. When is it permissible to put coffins and bodies on display in museums? After they have been buried ten years? One hundred? One thousand? How does this ethical issue relate to the U.S. federal Native American Repatriation Act, which requires that human bodies and religious artifacts of Native Americans be returned to their respective tribes?

Suggested Resources

In recent years, there has been a renewed interest in the art and culture of ancient Egypt. You will have no trouble obtaining posters and prints of such subjects as the Pyramids at Giza, the treasures of Tutankhamen's tomb, or genre scenes from tomb paintings.

EGYPTIAN FIGURE PAINTINGS

There are myriad possible projects for a culminating activity on Egyptian art, from building sugar-cube pyramids to making beaded jewelry. You can even buy modern papyrus sheets for art or hieroglyphics projects. I have chosen to focus on figure painting.

Materials tip: I do this project life-sized or larger, but you could certainly use 9" x 12" or 12" x 18" construction paper for a shorter-term project.

Procedure

1. I begin by creating a silhouette of each student on a piece of paper. Be sure the silhouette is "bald" and has a neck. (Also be sure to write the student's name on it.) There are several ways to do this:

    > I use the old-fashioned technique: Tape a sheet of paper to a wall in a small room that can be darkened. Have a student stand sideways with his or her shoulder pressed firmly to the paper, and shine a strong light on the student's head so that a clear profile is cast upon the center of the page. Then trace the profile of the head and neck with a pencil. (This is harder than it sounds, because students have a tendency to sway. You will want to practice in advance.)

    > Alternatively, take a profile shot of each student using a digital camera, print the results, and enlarge the print on a copy machine to the desired size. Simply cut out the copy and trace it onto the paper.

Instructional tip: Of course, you could merely provide each student with a generic head. I find, however, that this project engages the students more when the faces are actually their own.

---

2. Provide a great many visual aids for students to use as models. Students who are waiting to have their silhouettes traced should look at visual resources and sketch their ideas on manila paper. Demonstrate the project with a generic silhouette before tracing the students' silhouettes, so pupils can start to work as soon as they receive their materials, rather than waiting for you to finish all the tracings.

Egyptian Figure Paintings

Lesson Summary

Using silhouettes of their own head and neck, students create Egyptian wall paintings displaying authentic headdresses and necklaces.

Purpose

To reinforce the study of Egyptian art and culture; to emphasize the fact that Egyptian artists had to follow rules; to integrate geometric concepts with art and social studies.

Materials

- ❑ a variety of Egyptian figures as visual aids
- ❑ manila or scrap paper
- ❑ 3' x 3' sheets of white paper (I cut from a roll)
- ❑ pencils
- ❑ rulers with holes along the length (e.g., for insertion in a notebook)
- ❑ yardsticks
- ❑ tempera paints, including metallic gold
- ❑ paintbrushes
- ❑ 18" strips of sturdy cardboard with a series of holes punched in (optional but highly recommended)
- ❑ portable floodlight or lamp with bright bulb
- ❑ masking tape
- ❑ digital camera (optional)
- ❑ copy machine (optional)
- ❑ compass (optional)

Optional materials for display:

- ❑ roll of brown kraft paper
- ❑ scissors
- ❑ sponge
- ❑ white tempera paint
- ❑ stapler

In your demonstration, emphasize the following points (see figure 16 below for an illustration):

- Egyptian culture was very hierarchical, and artists had to follow rigid rules about certain things. For this project, you are the pharaoh who is giving them the rules they must follow.

- As in all Egyptian wall paintings, the eye should face out to the viewer. (Egyptians painted all body parts in the most easily and quickly recognizable position. Thus, although the face is drawn in profile, the eye is drawn from the front.)

- Position the front of the eye in the "dent" where the forehead and nose meet, not up in the forehead.

- Students may choose any appropriate headdress from a wig to a linen coif to a crown to a bald head. They may wear the false beard of a pharaoh. (Queen Hatshepset wore one during her reign, so girls may have beards if they wish.)

- In much Egyptian art, females were painted using an ocher (yellowish) color, whereas males were depicted in a reddish brown hue. (If you have access to multicultural paints, you might check out the *bronze* and *mahogany* tones.)

- Most figures in Egyptian wall paintings who wear jewelry wear necklaces reflecting the society's worship of the sun. If taken off and laid flat, the beads and other decorations on these pieces radiate out from the central hole like the rays of the sun.

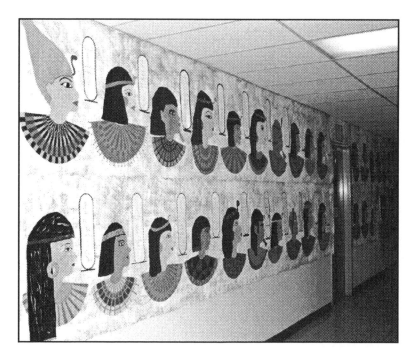

Figure 16. Egyptian wall paintings are displayed against a background of sponge-painted kraft paper.

3. **Optional step:** I insist that students' necklaces be geometrically perfect, and because I am pharaoh, what I say goes! If you wish to have students create geometrically perfect necklaces (a useful math exercise), here is the procedure:

- Students first draw a line with a ruler across the very top of the neck, from the base of the skull to immediately under the chin.

- They measure this line and place a dot at the midpoint (see figure 17a). This is the central point from which the necklace radiates. A lot depends on this point, so encourage them to be as accurate as possible.

- They place the point of a sharpened pencil through a hole at one end of a ruler, then place the pencil and ruler on the dot in the middle of the neck. Holding the pencil firmly in place, they insert a second pencil through the hole at the other end of the ruler. They move the second pencil to create an arc on the paper. (The ruler keeps the two pencils at a uniform distance, so the pencil will automatically move in an arc.) This forms the bottom of the necklace (see figure 17b).

Instructional tip: If students are working on 9" x 12" paper, a compass will probably be adequate to create the arc. If the scale of their drawing is such that they want an even deeper necklace than they can create with a ruler, they can simply punch holes in a strip of heavy cardboard (see figure 17c).

- Keeping the first pencil in place, students move the second to a hole much closer to the center dot. They make a second arc that just barely clears the sides of the neck (making sure it *does* clear the neck) for the top of the necklace (see figure 17c). They should now have two concentric arcs.

- Using a ruler or yardstick, they make a straight line from the dot in the middle of the neck to the end of the arc behind the head (forming the back shoulder). This line can be almost parallel to the bottom of the page, but should point somewhat downward.

- For the front of the necklace, they draw a line from the dot at the middle of the neck to the outside arc at an angle of 30–45 degrees below horizontal. Warn students not to draw a single line for the front and back of the necklace because it should be less than a semicircle (see figure 17d).

- Students may now divide the necklace geometrically in any way they desire to create decorations. They might make more concentric circles to divide the piece into different bands. They could place dots equidistant around the circumference of the outer circle—perhaps an inch apart on full-sized projects—and connect each dot with the center point, to create radiating strands. The necklace can be simple or as complex as time, skill, and geometry allow, but all designs must project radially from the central dot. Thus, a straight checkerboard pattern would not be acceptable, but one created from concentric circles and lines radiating from the center is fine. Students might fill the shapes that result from such a method with circles or connect the corners within each shape to create small triangles.

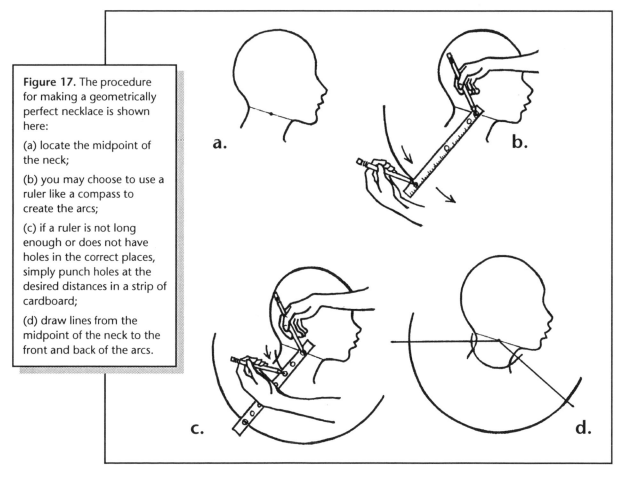

Figure 17. The procedure for making a geometrically perfect necklace is shown here:

(a) locate the midpoint of the neck;

(b) you may choose to use a ruler like a compass to create the arcs;

(c) if a ruler is not long enough or does not have holes in the correct places, simply punch holes at the desired distances in a strip of cardboard;

(d) draw lines from the midpoint of the neck to the front and back of the arcs.

a.

b.

c.

d.

4. After students have penciled in the necklace, have them pencil in lips, eyebrows, and ears (if they show). Be sure they erase any unnecessary lines before painting, so these do not show in the final project (some paints are not sufficiently opaque to cover pencil marks).

5. Finally, students paint their silhouette. Metallic gold tempera adds a nice touch for necklaces and jewelry. As the last step, lips and eyes should be outlined in black.

6. **Optional step:** When the pieces are dry, I cut out the figures and mount them in a class register on the hall walls (see figure 16). When I first started this project, I created a background using appropriate lengths of three-foot-wide kraft paper. I texturized it by dipping a large sponge lightly in white tempera and "printing" a mottled background over the entire surface. This background has lasted several years. Even if it rips, the tear merely adds to the aura of antiquity. I simply staple the students' paintings to it.

EGYPTIAN CARTOUCHES

The figure painting project takes several periods and students work at different paces, so I offer a supplementary lesson. Those who finish early may create a cartouche (an oval or oblong figure containing a pharaoh's name) of their name in hieroglyphs to hang next to their silhouette. Since certain letters do not appear in the Egyptian symbol system, finding a combination that comes close to the student's name can sometimes be a challenge. Rather than labeling each work in English, I mount a copy of the hieroglyph chart in the hall near the finished project and allow the passersby to try to figure out who's who.

Suggested Resources

Several sources, even entire books, are available on the Egyptian hieroglyphic system. Modern translators have added some vowels, which did not exist in Egyptian times. I use *The Dwellers on the Nile: The Life, History, Religion, and Literature of the Ancient Egyptians,* by E. A. Wallis Budge, to create a code for translating the hieroglyphs.

EGYPTIAN SCARABS

Another possible project for an Egyptian unit is to create scarabs. Because dung beetles seemed to generate spontaneously from decaying refuse, they were considered a symbol of life by early Egyptians.

Procedure

1. Using pictures as a guide, students model scarabs out of any appropriate material—clay, papier-mâché, plaster, dough—and inscribe their cartouches on the bottom.

2. They paint or glaze the dried scarab a turquoise blue to approximate the faience material the Egyptians frequently used for these charms. (Or you could use real faience, which is still available.)

Classical Greece and Rome

Among the lessons you might choose for a project on the Classical period are sculpture, pottery, models of buildings using columns or arch and vault construction, jewelry, and fresco (painting in wet plaster). There are also puzzles and cardboard models that depict famous architecture.

Due to time constraints and because the Romans copied so much of Greek art, I explore each of these cultures in depth but do only one of the following projects in any given year. (You could easily modify them and do both.) The Theater Masks project could be limited to Greek theater, and the Paper Mosaics lesson is essentially Roman in nature. Both require some ability to draw realistically. Hellenic art (Greek art before Alexander the Great) reflected the Greek philosophies of rationalism, humanism, and idealism, concepts suited to a culture experimenting with a new type of political structure, democracy. Figures were drawn to fit mathematical concepts of perfect proportions and stressed generic rather than individual traits. Even after Alexander, when Greek art became more realistic and expressive in nature, subject matter was treated in a naturalistic way, and the Roman art that followed focused a great deal on portraiture and the illusion of reality. I also try to focus on these concepts, although I allow room for the creative depiction of certain characters.

Suggested Resources

For visual aids, you might choose anything from Greek architecture such as the Parthenon, to Greek sculptures such as *The Discus Thrower, Doryphorus, Laocoön* (a nice gory one), or *The Winged Nike of Samothrace (Winged Victory)*. Roman choices could include the Colosseum, the Pantheon, the Pont du Gard, or the statue of Marcus Aurelius.

THEATER MASKS

My students learn about Greek comedy and tragedy as part of their language arts studies. You might want to make this a truly interdisciplinary project by studying history, art, and language arts simultaneously. As an art project, I keep the parameters pretty broad. I do not require my students to select a character from an actual play, but rather to limit themselves to subjects appropriate to Classical Greek or Roman civilization. Thus, they have chosen to depict everything from the Nemean lion, to gladiators, Cyclopes, soldiers, the wolf that suckled Romulus and Remus, Pegasus, and frogs from Aristophanes' *The Frogs*. Nymphs, gods, and goddesses are also very popular (see figure 18).

Figure 18. Greek theater mask projects show surprising diversity.

Instructional tip: There are a huge variety of ways to create masks. If your time is limited or you are not confident of your modeling abilities, you could do something as simple as having students draw the character on the convex side of a paper plate or even on a piece of cardboard, which eliminates the three-dimensional challenge.

Procedure

1. For a simple human face using a round plate, have students make a cut about 1½″ long along a radius from the outer edge of the plate toward the center. They overlap the two cut edges and staple. The cut section will project out from the rest of the plate, creating a chin.

2. Students cut a rectangle of cardboard about ⅓ as long as the diameter of the plate and about 2″ to 3″ wide.

3. They fold the cardboard in half lengthwise and cut from the outside bottom corner to the fold at the top (see figure 19). The resulting triangle with a fold down the middle will be the basis of the nose. Spreading the halves of the triangle apart somewhat, they center the nose on the plate with the apex of the triangle at the top. They attach the nose with masking tape along the sides.

Theater Masks
Lesson Summary

Students create masks with three-dimensional features, depicting any animal or person known to the Greeks (or possibly the Romans). After creating the basic form, or armature, from a paper plate and cardboard, they coat with plaster gauze and paint in lifelike colors.

Purpose

To give students experience with three-dimensional challenges; to reinforce study of Classical Greek and Roman cultures; possibly to use for further integration in a play.

Materials

- ❑ sturdy round and oval paper plates, such as Chinette
- ❑ stapler
- ❑ scissors
- ❑ utility knives (optional)
- ❑ rolls of 1″ masking tape
- ❑ poster board or railroad board
- ❑ plaster gauze or papier-mâché
- ❑ tempera or acrylic paint and paintbrushes
- ❑ lots of newspaper (optional for making three-dimensional masks)
- ❑ decorations such as feathers, yarn, shells

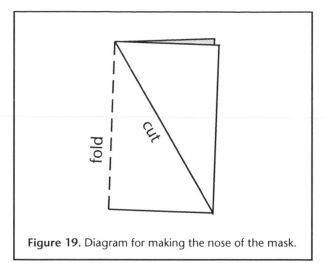

Figure 19. Diagram for making the nose of the mask.

4. If you are actually planning to use the masks for performance purposes, have students draw the eyes on the plate and cut them out before building the rest of the form. Otherwise, the eyes can be painted on after the mask is plastered

5. To complete the mask, students cut out and tape on cardboard ears, cover the form with papier-mâché or plaster gauze, paint the result, and decorate.

Instructional tips: If you have art training, you could demonstrate how to use wadded-up newspaper armatures and plaster gauze to create cheeks, a forehead, and eyes for more lifelike faces (see figure 18). Ensure that students tape the forms smoothly in place with masking tape before covering with papier-mâché or plaster gauze.

This project offers a chance to stress human proportions and incorporate math learning. The Greeks followed mathematical guidelines to create ideal relationships in their figures. Even after the advent of Alexander, when Greek art became more realistic, certain conventions prevailed, just as they do in realistic drawing and sculpting today. Briefly, from the hairline to the base of the chin, the face can be divided into thirds. The tops of the eyelids are located $\frac{1}{3}$ of the distance down from the hairline to the chin. The eyes should be spaced so there is room for one eye between them. The nose occupies the center $\frac{1}{3}$ of the face, beginning between the eyes. The lowest $\frac{1}{3}$ of the face contains the mouth and chin. You might want to watch a video or scan a text on facial proportions. Better yet, coordinate with a science teacher to teach students the basic anatomy of the human skull and facial musculature.

PAPER MOSAICS

Procedure

1. As always, start by showing a wide variety of slides, videos, or filmstrips, and have several visual aids available as students are working.

2. Discuss the way Romans placed their tiles. Unlike modern mosaics, the tesserae (that is, mosaic tiles) were arranged in very regular rows and were generally square, although of course the students may cut pieces to fit. Since the goal is to approximate a real mosaic, made from ceramic tiles embedded in plaster, none of the tesserae may overlap.

3. Have the students sketch their ideas on scratch paper first. Review the designs for authenticity, good composition, and practicality (small details will be very difficult in a mosaic technique). I require students to portray a type of image that a Roman would have chosen and present it in a Roman way: animals, fruits, vegetables, or other plants that Romans of the day would have known about; people such as gladiators, senators, philosophers, soldiers, women, and Roman gods and goddesses; buildings; geometric floor designs; and so on. Fish and sea creatures are very popular subjects (see figure 20), as are bridges and aqueducts. Greek imagery is fine, since so much of Roman art was based on Greek prototypes.

Instructional tip: The requirement of authenticity can be a wonderful catalyst for research. I once had a student who wanted to depict bowling pins in his mosaic. He found that Roman rulers bowled with ivory pins and Egyptian pharaohs had ones of gold. I have had students check the geographical distribution of various animals, to make sure they would have been known to the Romans.

---

4. Once their designs have been approved, students sketch them lightly with a pencil on a piece of sturdy gray cardboard.

Paper Mosaics

Lesson Summary

Using cardboard and colored paper, students create mosaics depicting any authentically Roman subject.

Purpose

To reinforce study of Roman (or Greek) art and culture; to inspire appreciation for the art and craft of mosaic work, which was a major art form in both Roman and Medieval times.

Materials

- ❏ various colors of construction paper or coated (i.e., shiny) paper, cut in $1/4$" squares
- ❏ small container to store each color of paper
- ❏ pencils
- ❏ sketch paper
- ❏ pieces of sturdy gray cardboard about 7" x 9"
- ❏ glue sticks (do not use liquid glue)
- ❏ damp paper towels for cleanup
- ❏ clear polymer sealant (optional)

5. Students cover a small area of the cardboard with glue stick (not liquid glue) and begin arranging the paper tiles, continuing until they cover the entire surface of the cardboard. Tiles should be spaced evenly, leaving a very small amount of cardboard showing between them to simulate the plaster or grout.

Instructional tips: Have students work with only one or two colors at a time, and encourage them to take only what they think they will need, to avoid mixing colors and values when returning unused tiles. Also encourage students to keep their hands clean and to avoid getting glue on the top of the tesserae.

---

6. The mosaics can be sprayed with a clear polymer to protect them and add sheen to the paper tiles.

Figure 20. Angela Ripani created this charming seahorse with a distinctly Roman style.

Variations

This project can be adapted in a number of ways. You could create real mosaics. Perhaps the entire class could design and create one large mosaic for your school, using an authentic theme and real tiles. You can order supplies from catalogs (see References and Resources) or check with local craft stores or flooring supply centers. You could work with the math teacher to create geometric designs such as tessellations (see page 150). For young children, you could make the squares much larger. Perhaps you could use M&Ms set in white icing on a cake to create a Greek pebble mosaic and then eat the results!

The Middle Ages

After the fall of the Roman Empire and the chaos that ensued, Western art reflected men and women's preoccupation with their souls and their preparations for a more pleasant afterlife. Christianity had become the dominant religion in Europe and Islam was on the rise in Africa and parts of Asia, so it is no surprise to find art history books filled with pictures of cathedrals and mosques, mosaics from these edifices, sculptures of religious figures, and illustrations from religious texts. I describe a manuscript illumination project on the following pages, but you could easily adapt the

Paper Mosaic lesson for this period. (Make some tesserae out of gold wrapping paper for a truly authentic feel.) Other possible lessons include tapestry projects such as needlepoint or embroidery, sculpture, actual calligraphy, painting on wood, woodcut prints, metal tooling, and various commercially available three-dimensional puzzles and models of Gothic or Romanesque cathedrals. In the Physics in Architecture section (page 129), I describe an exercise that helps students understand the development of flying buttresses, which I present during my unit on the Middle Ages.

 ### Suggested Resources

For a study of medieval architecture, *Nôtre Dame: Cathedral of Amiens* is a wonderful video set that shows a walk through this lovely Gothic structure (part 1) and a discussion of its architecture, although one of the videos might be too slow for younger students. Part 2, *Revelation—Computer and Architectural Animation*, presents a truly outstanding discussion of the architectural and philosophical beauties of this marvelous building, and it can be purchased separately. (Note that this is not the famous Nôtre Dame Cathedral in Paris, which is another fine example of High Gothic architecture. You can certainly find posters of either cathedral to hang in your room.)

MANUSCRIPT ILLUMINATION

A faux manuscript illumination is a fairly straightforward but effective way to wrap up a study of the Medieval period. Since Medieval artists were generally less interested in showing the physical realities of this world than in expressing spiritual truths, you need not worry about being able to draw accurately. Indeed, you should emphasize the distortions and styles of the period, providing lots of visual aids.

Manuscript Illumination
Lesson Summary

Students pick a Latin, Hebrew, Greek, Arabic, or Cyrillic letter (or very short word). They produce a highly decorated, or illuminated, letter on parchment paper, mimicking authentic styles from the Middle Ages.

Purpose

To reinforce the study of Medieval art and culture; to inspire appreciation for the craft of illumination; to focus on the expressionistic fervor of the Middle Ages.

Materials

❑ manila paper or other inexpensive paper
❑ pencils
❑ rulers
❑ colored pencils (optional)
❑ 11" x 14" calligraphic parchment paper (sold in tablets of 50)
❑ various colors of tempera (or watercolors or colored markers)
❑ gold color, preferably tempera or paint pens (or gold crayons or pencils)
❑ several sizes of paintbrushes
❑ fine-tipped black markers

Suggested Resources

The Lindisfarne Gospels and the Book of Kells are famous illuminated Latin manuscripts, but there are exquisite texts in Hebrew and Arabic as well.

Procedure

1. Begin with a slide and video introduction to the various styles of texts produced in the Middle Ages. You may wish to show examples of texts using the Latin alphabet in upper and lower case (it was during the Medieval period that *minuscule* letters were introduced), as well as Greek, Arabic, Hebrew, and Cyrillic texts. Point out that even in modern books, the first letter of a chapter or a paragraph may be very large and fancy, a legacy of Medieval scribes.

2. Discuss the various methods of decorating letters. Some letters are just extremely fancy, embellished with vines, knot designs, or animal interlace motifs. In other cases, the letter is actually made up of animals, plants, buildings, or some such device. Also point out the extreme distortion of many of the figures and how fanciful some of the imagery is.

3. Explain that students are to choose one letter from any appropriate alphabet and illuminate it in an authentic way. Clarify that Chinese characters, Egyptian hieroglyphics, and other letters not in use in Medieval Europe are not appropriate. Explain that in this context *illuminate* means to decorate. Then show previous students' works in various stages of completion, to demonstrate the project.

Instructional tip: This project can offer wonderful possibilities to your more creative students while allowing those with less fertile imaginations to produce pieces equally beautiful in their own way. I encourage students to stick with a single letter, but I have accepted very short words in the past.

---

4. Once students have chosen their letter, (usually an initial), they do a rough sketch on manila paper. Have students place a ruler with the outer edge on the edge of the paper and draw a very light pencil line along the inner edge. They repeat this process on all sides to create a border a ruler's width wide. The letter and any background must fit within the border so that some parchment will show on all finished projects.

5. Within the image area, students may choose whether to enclose the letter in a solid painted background or simply have the parchment be the background. They may draw an oval, circle, diamond, or shield-shaped background. If they choose a geometric pattern for the

background, such as diamonds or a checkerboard, it must be even and uniform. You may wish to demonstrate the easiest and quickest way to do this, as follows.

For a diamond pattern: Place your ruler diagonally from one corner of the border to the opposite corner and draw a pencil line. Repeat with the remaining two corners to create a large X. Lay your ruler along one line of the X and draw a parallel line a ruler's width away. Then lay your ruler on the second line and repeat the process. Continue both above and below each line of the X until you have filled the page with diamonds.

For a checkerboard: Place a dot exactly halfway across each line of the border. Connect the opposing dots to divide the background in half both vertically and horizontally. (You should have four equal quarters.) Lay the ruler on the vertical center line and make a parallel line a ruler's width away. Lay the ruler on the second line and draw another line. Repeat this process both vertically and horizontally until your checkerboard is complete.

Figure 21. Fifth grader Lindsey Garrison added fine details such as patterns for fish scales and water in this lovely manuscript illumination.

6. Once you have approved a student's design, give him or her a piece of parchment. The student draws the design lightly in pencil on the parchment, then begins painting it in. For images that include a person, I have students leave the skin unpainted so that the parchment color serves as a flesh tone. Gold paint should be used effectively, not overdone.

7. All black lines are put in with a fine line marker after the paint is dry. This makes painting easier in some cases. For instance, if students are creating leaves, they simply paint a flat green shape and, when it is dry, outline it and add the vein lines with marker. Details of faces, fish or dragon scales, blocks on a castle wall, and so on, all are added on top of the dry paint. Virtually every element is outlined (see figure 21).

Variation

For a variation on this idea, see the Music Manuscript Illumination lesson on page 163.

The Renaissance

As Europe developed increasing stability, the people had more time to develop interests beyond physical or spiritual survival. The Black Death and the Reformation changed the prevailing attitude about religious matters, and new discoveries and inventions helped change their worldview as well. The influx of scholars into Italy following the fall of Constantinople spurred a resurgence of interest in Classical Greek texts and the philosophies of idealism, rationalism, and humanism. These philosophies as well as the blossoming interest in the physical world combined to yield the art of the Renaissance, with its focus on scientifically accurate portrayals and the affairs of humankind as well as religion.

You are probably quite familiar with Renaissance art, including paintings and sculptures by Michelangelo Buonarroti, Leonardo da Vinci, Raphael Sanzio or Santi (Raphael), Donatello, Sandro Botticelli, Albrecht Dürer, or Jan van Eyck. The Sistine Chapel and the *Mona Lisa* are certainly well known. I give students a broad overview of the famous works of this era, but my projects explore the development of *perspective,* the various rules for portraying the illusion of distance and three-dimensionality accurately on a two-dimensional surface. An increasingly three-dimensional view of the world required an increasingly three-dimensional means of communication.

Perspective can be described as *point of view.* The contours of virtually all forms except a sphere change when we change our position. Some earlier cultures, such as the Greeks and Romans, had created works that portrayed space fairly well. Indeed, the Romans came very close to reality in some cases. Other societies, such as the Egyptians, most Medieval cultures, African cultures, and the indigenous cultures in the Americas, had little interest in formulating mathematical rules for the accurate depiction of forms in space. Their philosophies dictated that their art serve other purposes. The Chinese and Japanese likewise had a different approach to reality, frequently using a device called *isometric perspective,* in which parallelograms are used to suggest the depth of buildings but there are no fixed horizon and vanishing point. However, the development in Renaissance Europe of the rules governing linear, circular, and aerial perspective was ultimately to have enormous impact upon the entire world, and the philosophy that an artist's primary goal was to create an illusion of reality dominated Western painting for the next five hundred years. You can do several exercises to introduce the concept of perspective to your students. See the Perspective section (pages 145–50), including the Still-Life project that culminates our Renaissance unit.

Suggested Resources

- I strongly recommend a wonderful video entitled *Masters of Illusion*. My students love it!
- For your own information, or to show your class, you might also check out the video *Art Is...Basic Perspective Drawing*.

The Seventeenth and Eighteenth Centuries

In Western art, the years from approximately 1600 to 1775 are referred to as the Baroque and Rococo periods. This was a lavish age of great contrasts, with increasing divisions among the rich and the poor, and of course these changes are reflected in the paintings, sculpture, architecture, and decorative arts of the time. To the upper classes, bigger was generally better: wider skirts, taller wigs, more enormous palaces and homes, larger canvases with more figures, and performing arts with more instruments, more dancers, and more singers. Expensive fabrics, elaborate carvings, gilt overlays, and valuable and exotic accessories all testified to the wealth and power of the privileged elite. Religion and morality continued to play a role (see the section on *vanitas* paintings on page 112). But the trend toward the enjoyment of earthly delights, which had blossomed during the Renaissance, continued. As the church finally yielded its position that the earth was the center of the universe, the new view of the vastness of the universe influenced wonderful landscape paintings and architectural settings in which the eye was drawn into the far distance. Although they imparted cautionary morals, still-life painters nonetheless focused on objects that only their wealthy patrons could afford, and the bulk of art served the purposes of the aristocracy, the church, and the state, or at least the very rich. It is not surprising, therefore, to find that portraiture, which had become popular during the Renaissance, was a premier form of visual art.

Suggested Resources

You might want to check out works by Peter Paul Rubens, Diego Velázquez (especially *Las Meninas*), Jan Vermeer, Jean-Antoine Watteau, Giovanni Antonio Canal (Canaletto), Jean Baptiste Simeon Chardin, Thomas Gainsborough, William Hogarth, (especially his series *Marriage à la Mode* and *The Rake's Progress*), or Rembrandt van Rijn.

We begin our culminating activities with the Split Face exercise described on page 139. This allows us to focus on real proportions, forms, and so forth. Since it follows our unit on perspective drawing and shading, it is a nice way to apply and reinforce what we have just learned. As students finish that exercise, they begin the final project, which is a full-sized self-portrait dressed appropriately for the era.

Self-Portrait

Lesson Summary

Students create life-sized self-portraits of themselves in dress appropriate to the seventeenth or eighteenth century.

Purpose

To reinforce study of the cultures of 1600 to 1775; to help personalize the time period; to inspire research; to learn about working in a large format; to reinforce and expand upon skills introduced in the Renaissance unit.

Materials

- ❑ visual aids showing clothing, costumes, and portraits from the era
- ❑ rolls of white paper 3' wide
- ❑ scissors
- ❑ pencils
- ❑ tempera or colored markers
- ❑ black background to mount the figures on for display (optional)

SELF-PORTRAIT

Because portraiture was an important feature of the Baroque and Rococo periods, this project makes a good finale. However, it can be adapted in very many ways for many different cultures and time periods, so you can set your own rules to suit your needs. My rules require that the students select a costume from the years 1600 to 1775, and that if they choose a particular ethnicity or native costume, it must represent their own heritage. That is, a student whose forebears all hailed from Scandinavia cannot decide to be a Native American. A student who has Native American ancestry, on the other hand, may choose to research the native dress of her particular tribe or opt to dress in European garb, as Pocahontas did when she visited the court of King James. Whatever the student decides, the result must be authentic and personal (see figure 22).

Materials tip: On the day they are to be traced the students must wear or bring clothing that allows for accurate outlining of their body, such as a basketball uniform, swim trunks, light T-shirt, or tank top. They may easily wear such clothing under their normal attire or change at school. Because women wore full skirts in those days, only the girls' top half and feet need be closely traced, unless they have chosen a costume that is form-fitting, such as an Indian sari.

Procedure

1. Cut a sheet of paper 7' long for each student. This allows room for headdresses, tall helmets, feathers, or other headgear.

2. Have each student in turn lie on a sheet of paper while you trace his or her outline. Unless you are a fairly competent artist, you will probably wish to have your students take a very simple pose, lying straight on the paper with their hands at their sides. You might also need someone's help roughing out the head and face area. The students will draw in their own features.

Instructional tip: It will take more than one period to trace all the students, so plan activities or independent work for the students who are waiting their turn.

3. Once his or her outline has been traced, each student must draw in the clothing and other details appropriately using pencil. Students frequently do research in addition to the sources I provide. Many of them bring in materials from home, such as Japanese artifacts, Scottish tartans, or information on how a young woman from India would have worn her hair.

4. Because I am teaching students art, I demonstrate how to use the tempera paint to make forms appear real. When students paint their self-portraits, I require them to use shading accurately. Because I cut out all the finished projects and mount them on a black background to approximate the huge canvases and chiaroscuro of the period, I specify the direction of the light source so that all the figures' shading will agree. (*Chiaroscuro*, literally "light dark" in Italian, refers to the modeling of objects in light and shadow.)

Figure 22. The father of artist Thomas Gonyea is a member of the Onondaga Indian Nation, Beaver Clan. The tattoos Gonyea portrays here are authentic for the period.

Instructional tip: This project takes a lot of time and floor space, so you may decide simply to have your students go over their pencil lines with markers. That way, you could use a gym or cafeteria floor without needing sinks or creating a lot of mess.

Variations

- Another approach to this project would be to have the students draw a famous person.
- As an independent assignment, I have students write an "autobiography" of the people they drew themselves as. I display these with the self-portraits (see the Autobiography lesson on page 108 for a description).
- Another alternative would be to pass out postcards of Baroque- and Rococo-period portraits and have each student create a "biography" of that individual, based not upon facts but upon an understanding of the times (see the Autobiography lesson on page 108).

The Age of Revolution

The century from 1775 to 1875 is sometimes referred to in art texts as the Age of Revolution. This period brought dramatic changes in politics, economics, civil rights, transportation, communication, and industry, and there was, not surprisingly, a concurrent upheaval in the art produced during that turbulent time. Philosophies splintered, creating new and conflicting movements in music, literature, and the visual arts. Some would say that this spirit of revolution continues to the present day.

The movements known as Neoclassicism, Romanticism, and Realism dominated Western art during that period, each a rebellion of sorts against prevailing modes. For the artist, all are important because they sum up, in a way, the approaches that artists take when interpreting a subject: rational (or analytic), emotional, and purely mimetic. These approaches would ultimately be intensified to yield such late-nineteenth and twentieth-century movements as Formalism (including Cubism, Futurism, Minimalism, and Constructivism), Expressionism (including Fauvism, Action Painting, and Abstract Expressionism), and Photorealism or Super-Realism.

Neoclassicism: The Neoclassicists focused on extremely precise renderings of subjects that extolled Classical virtues and historical grandeur. Works by artists such as Jacques-Louis David glorified patriotism, civic duty, bravery, and noble leadership. You might want to check out such pieces as *The Oath of the Horatii, The Death of Socrates,* and *The Death of Marat,* all by David, to get a feel for this style. You will note that the stable, simplified compositions offer a strong contrast to the swirling opulence of so many Baroque canvases. Examples from architecture are equally instructive. Our founding fathers chose designs that incorporated Greek columns and facades to symbolize the democratic nature of the fledgling nation, whereas Napoleon dotted his landscape with triumphal arches, domes, and columns that called to mind the might of Rome.

Romanticism: The Romantic movement also focused upon conveying messages of virtue, but the content and manner of delivery were somewhat different. The brushwork and even the subject matter tended to be far more emotional, frequently extolling the cleansing properties of nature as well as such concepts as democracy, liberty, and human rights. Considering the problems raised by the industrial age with its attendant slums and abuses of the workers, such imagery is not surprising. Works by Joseph Mallord William Turner, Francisco de Goya, Théodore Géricault, John Constable, Honoré Daumier, and Eugène Delacroix will illustrate this approach. In Britain especially, architects emulated ancient Gothic modes as an atmospheric alternative to the Roman styles chosen by their French foes and the Greek designs used by the upstart former colonies.

Realism: The Realists espoused quite a different philosophy from the other artists of their day. They felt that art should focus on the "realities" of life, without romanticizing them or ascribing artificially noble interpretations to them. The subjects they chose—including prostitutes, laborers, beggars, and funerals—were not popular with most critics or patrons. The paintings of Gustave Courbet, especially *Burial at Ornans* and *The Artist's Studio,* are premier examples of this genre.

Several technological advances occurred during this period that were to have far-ranging implications for artists. Among these was the invention of the collapsible tin for holding paints. Before this development, oil paints were carried in bulky animal bladders. Because transporting paints was a problem, artists usually did preliminary sketches outdoors and created the final painting from those sketches in the artificial environment of their studio. The new containers made it feasible for artists to paint on location under actual conditions of changing light and weather. They began to notice even more clearly how such changes affected the scene before them, and this new perception would be one of several important factors in the rise of the Impressionist movement.

AGE OF REVOLUTION PROJECT IDEAS

Since painting outdoors (*en pleine aire*) was an important development of the Age of Revolution, we do an outdoor project as our culminating activity for this unit. We simply take pencils, paper, and drawing boards (corrugated cardboard) outside and draw trees. If the location of your school makes this an impossibility, you could choose some other subject. You will also need a backup activity if the weather does not cooperate. For example, I have students obtain color photographs or prints of real trees. I also have a large supply of such references on hand. Calendars and library books are good sources for such visuals.

It is preferable to do this project over several days so that you can take advantage of changes in light quality. If the same class meets at different times on different days of the week, encourage students to notice how the position of the sun affects shadows and colors. If your room allows students to draw while looking out a window, you could do this project in the winter when trees are bare. If you are lucky enough to have snow, watching the way it reflects different kinds of light can be very educational.

Of course, you can finish your projects in different ways. We usually leave ours as drawings, but you could do light pencil outlines, color the trunks and certain other details heavily with wax crayon, and paint over this with a watercolor wash (a very watery, thin layer of paint) for the sky. When this is dry, use a small piece of sponge dipped in tempera or watercolor to "print" the leaves. Remember to mix colors.

There are several other projects you could do for this time period. Your students could do a drawing illustrating a current event that contains a moral or one designed to elicit sympathy for an actual situation. You could use paintings such as David's series chronicling Napoleon's coronation or his *The Death of Marat*, Goya's *The Third of May 1808*, or Géricault's *The Raft of the Medusa* to inspire research or discussion about the era.

1875 to the Present

Over the last 125 years, art theories have come and gone at a dizzying pace (see figure 23). Even Impressionism—probably one of the most popular and recognized movements in the entire history of art—lasted only about fifteen years. Indeed, it might be interpreted as one more revolution in the Age of Revolution. As a result of a variety of factors—the invention of the camera, discoveries about the physics of light, the development of cadmium colors, improvements in transportation, the theories of Darwin and Freud, and the invention of the collapsible tin, to name a few—artists began focusing on different qualities in their works, among them the changing nature of light. Artists had used light to show more about a subject for hundreds of years. Now, however, they began using the subject to show more about the light. Claude Monet was not actually painting wheat stacks or water lilies or Rouen cathedral. He was merely using them to show how light changed our perception of them at different times of the day or year or under different weather conditions.

> *"People are thinking that art is drawing pictures with crayons and markers and paint. Art is a way of expressing oneself."*
>
> —Matt, Sycamore student

For much of the Classical era and certainly from the Renaissance through most of the 1800s, Western visual artists had focused their energies on creating the illusion of physical reality. In many cases, this effort was combined with a desire to capture psychological, religious, or spiritual reality as well, but whatever the message was, it was delivered in a language everyone could understand. With the invention of the camera—and even more revolutionary, the movie camera—many artists began questioning whether the imitation of reality should really be their primary objective. After all, mechanical devices could now capture the physical world in the most realistic manner possible. Sculptors—at least before Alexander Calder invented the mobile—were limited to solid, unmoving materials, and painters, despite the most exacting perspective, could not create a better illusion of three dimensions on their two-dimensional surfaces than a photographer could. Indeed, several painters turned to photography, both as an art form in itself and to aid them in painting. In the latter part of the nineteenth century, Paul Cézanne opened the door to a new structuring of space with compositions that did not follow the rules of perspective. Painters stopped trying to fool the eye into ignoring the flatness and solidity of the canvas or the wall and started to emphasize these qualities instead. Coincident with new theories about space and time, they created works that depicted the subject viewed simultaneously from different points of view. Influenced by a new interest in African masks and sculpture, they adopted the simplification and abstraction that lent such power to those objects, and they continued Cézanne's efforts to bring the background forward and push the foreground back.

Some artists, such as Pablo Picasso and Georges Braque, applied these new theories in a relatively detached, analytical way that became known as Cubism, whereas others, such as Henri Matisse, used color and line more expressively in a style called Fauvism,

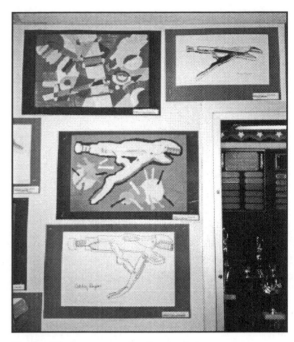

Figure 23. For our study of twentieth-century art, students bring in an object which they treat in a variety of styles. Here Ashley Raynor has created a wrench using Cubism, Realism, and Expressionism, as well as contour drawing.

but ultimately the approaches overlapped. Other artists adapted some of these conventions to their own purposes. Thus the works of the European and Mexican Expressionist movements, which used art to focus attention on political and social problems, used media, elements, and principles in a highly emotional way as well as showing the effects of Cubism.

Because artists are significantly affected by the social, political, technological, and economic realities of their times, it is very easy to find twentieth-century art movements to illuminate and reinforce the teaching of history. It is also important to be aware of the cultural events that shaped artworks. The stock market crash and the Depression, for example, spawned various reactions on the part of artists. Some, such as the Regionalists, chose to create works focusing on the enduring values of American life. Grant Wood and Thomas Hart Benton painted scenes of people, the land, and industry with fertile fields, hard-working individuals, and productive factories. Conversely, Social Realists such as Ben Shahn used art to spotlight contemporary issues and problems, such as soup lines, the Dust Bowl, and McCarthyism. The earlier Dada movement had been started by a group of artists and writers protesting World War I, and one of its principal proponents, Marcel Duchamp, later influenced Pop and Conceptual Art. Studying the Futurists would be a great way to reinforce a lesson on how

> "(Art education) may not make a person a better artist in general, but for most people, I think it improves or enriches their lives."
>
> —Andrea, Sycamore student

mechanical innovations such as the automobile, train, and so on have affected our culture. (Unlike most creative people, Futurists looked upon these advances as positive influences. Their views and how they differed from the majority opinion would make a great subject for a debate.)

Other historical tie-ins include how Diego Rivera used his murals and paintings to protest conditions in Mexico, and certainly how Adolf Hitler castigated the "degenerate" artists (virtually anyone who did not create realistic works glorifying the Third Reich) and eventually drove them out of Germany. For a truly fascinating story of an artist standing firm against the Nazis, study the life and works of Kathe Kollwitz. Exploring Socialist Realist art (not to be confused with Social Realism) can be a wonderful way to illuminate the early history of the USSR, and one could learn a great deal about China under Mao Tse-Tung by studying how art fared during the Cultural Revolution. Indeed, it is interesting to note that dictators inevitably place limitations on art, whether those dictators are Egyptian pharaohs, Nazi fuehrers, or Communist chairmen.

Another influence reflected in the art of the last 125 years is the study of psychology and the subconscious engendered by the work of people such as Freud and Jung. To spur discussion about how theories in psychology and psychiatry have affected everything from popular culture to education to law, examine pieces by Expressionists such as Max Beckmann or Emil Nolde, earlier works by Edvard Munch or James Ensor, and examples of Fantasy Art and Surrealism by such artists as Salvador Dali, René Magritte, Paul Klee, or Marc Chagall.

As time progressed, artists looked for more ways to express the qualities that made a work of art unique. Removing anything that could be considered the rightful province of some other discipline—morals, storytelling, musical allusions, imagery—left the artist with essentially pure elements and principles. In works of the Suprematist, Formalist, Color-Field, Large-Field, and Minimalist movements, color, shape, texture, value, line, and form became ends in themselves. They belonged only to the realm of visual arts and could not be co-opted by ruling groups to serve any other purpose. Abstract Expressionism was touted as the art of the new Utopia. Still, although proponents such as Jackson Pollock and Willem de Kooning have earned solid places in the history of art, Abstract Expressionism is quietly becoming just one more "ism" in an age of "isms."

Conceptualism was perhaps the most confusing (and for many infuriating) theory to arise in recent times. For people who saw red every time they found a blank white canvas hanging in a museum, Conceptual Art was the final straw. Ever since the Impressionists stopped hiding the action of painting from the viewer (that is, you are aware of every brush stroke), the *process* of creating the art began gaining more and more importance until Conceptualism postulated that the process was more important than the product. The idea or concept behind the work, the action of creating the vehicle, and the action of viewing or listening to it—many felt that this was where the art resided. Once the action was complete, the "visual residue" could be discarded. When Marcel Duchamp painted a mustache and beard on a copy of the *Mona Lisa* and exhibited a urinal he titled *Fountain,* he inspired an entirely new group of artists whose *raison d'être* became making people question the nature of art. At a time when art theories that had stood for 500 years were being challenged, perhaps such a movement was inevitable.

Suggested Resources

- If you are interested in a brilliant yet accessible discussion of contemporary art, read *After the End of Art* by Arthur Danto.
- Everyone interested in the cultural history of the United States would profit by reading *Life, The Movie* by Neal Gabler.

PROJECTS FOR CONTEMPORARY ART

You will notice that I have not suggested hands-on activities to accompany these art movements. The projects that I do in my class truly require an art teacher, and such specialists are familiar with a wealth of projects appropriate to the time. Here are some alternatives other teachers might consider:

Pinhole cameras: For Impressionism, why not have your students make pinhole cameras? You could collaborate with the art or science teacher on this project, or get a how-to book from the library. Certain software programs, such as Adobe Photoshop, have features that can interpret scanned or digital photos in broken color or pointillism.

Posters of social issues: For twentieth-century Realism in the context of a history class, it might be most beneficial to concentrate on Social Realism, the Regionalists, or even Socialist Realism. You could have the students do posters or photographs that focus on a current event or social issue. In fact, this would be a great opportunity to explore the works of Dorothea Lange or Margaret Bourke-White or photojournalism in general.

Socially conscious art: You might prefer to have your students study the works of Kathe Kollwitz or Diego Rivera and produce expressive pieces that deal with emotion-laden current issues.

Integrated humanities studies: Music often reflects the social issues of the time. Everything from folk music to the popular music of the Depression to rap contains references to contemporary events and problems. Several teachers could collaborate in an interdisciplinary project that would illustrate the time under discussion by studying music, art, and literature that relate to it. Examples for the Depression era might be *The Grapes of Wrath* by John Steinbeck, the song "Brother, Can You Spare a Dime?" by E. Y. Harburg and Jay Gorney, and artworks by Ben Shahn.

Videos and advertising: For a lesson integrating your subject with Pop Art, you might explore any contemporary medium such as video or advertising. ❧

> *"My artwork has also helped me in other subjects such as history. The artwork from the time really shows you how different people felt about different things . . . you feel closer to the people of the time."*
> —Alyssa, Sycamore student

CHAPTER 10
Language Arts

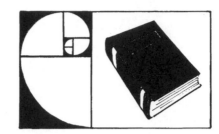

"As images become cheap, words tend to be crowded out. "
—Edmund Burke Feldman

Art can be an invaluable tool for the language arts teacher, especially in conjunction with creative writing. In recent years, the written word has actually been incorporated into Western art. Roy Lichtenstein, the Pop artist who created paintings based upon comic book imagery, and Post-Modernist Conceptual artists Barbara Kruger and Jenny Holzer are good examples of this phenomenon. Faith Ringgold's story quilts would be wonderful artifacts upon which to base an integrated unit. The next few lesson plans offer a variety of ways in which teachers can use works of art or thoughts about the nature of art to inspire written and visual work.

Creative Writing

Works of art are wonderful starting points for the creation of poetry. I have used the following method, which is based on a suggestion I heard at a Getty conference some years ago, in my eighth-grade class with terrific results. You could easily use it in this form for high school or college students, and with modifications, primarily of subject matter, it could be adapted for children as young as kindergarten.

Suggested Resources

For this project I recommend selecting an artwork that is ambiguous enough to yield multiple interpretations. You might want to consider works by Kathe Kollwitz, Audrey Flack, Katsushika Hokusai, Edward Hopper, Max Beckmann, René Magritte, Jacob Lawrence, or Henri Rousseau. I have had wonderful results with the painting *Into the World Came a Soul Called Ida* by Ivan Albright, and there is great scope for interpretation in certain African sculptures and Moslem manuscript illuminations.

Word Lists and Poetry

Lesson Summary

Students brainstorm a list of words to describe a piece of art. Then, after further analysis, they use the list as a basis for writing prose or poetry about the piece.

Purpose

To encourage students to truly attend to the work of art under discussion; to engage students in a very nonthreatening way; to lead them to notice details in the work that they might otherwise have overlooked; to expand their vocabulary and general powers of observation.

Materials

- ❑ work of art
- ❑ a way to display the artwork to the class (e.g., slide projector, overhead projector, easel)
- ❑ chalkboard and chalk
- ❑ notebooks and pencils

WORD LISTS AND POETRY

The creation of a word list, as described below, can be a valuable tool in and of itself. Language arts teachers can use the exercise in a variety of ways to expand vocabulary or discuss types of words or nuance, or simply to help pupils be more observant. Perhaps students could carry a notebook and get into the habit of generating personal word lists as an exercise to improve their descriptive writing skills. What about having students create a word list on the school bus or at the mall or while watching a television show? Such an exercise could help students analyze their feelings and perceptions. What about an integrated language and art assignment? Before or after sketching a scene or still life or figure, the student could fill the facing page in the sketchbook with word associations germane to the experience. The words could reflect the artist's feelings at the time, qualities of the subject matter, or references to related works. Perhaps the word list itself could be woven into the artwork in a creative way. The possibilities are endless.

Procedure

1. Choose an artwork. Any work of art will do, but those with ambiguity yield the most interesting results.

    Instructional tip: You will find it beneficial to do some background research on the selected piece so you can lead an informed discussion. Several books with instructive annotations are listed in the References and Resources.

    ---

2. Place the piece where the entire group can see it. A large art print or poster would work, as would a slide. Several small reproductions, such as postcards, to share among small groups are fine, as long as the students can see details clearly and everyone is viewing the same image. At this point, the only information I give the class is the title and the artist's name.

3. Start by generating a word list. Ask each student to contribute a word or short phrase that occurs to him or her on viewing this image. List students' ideas on the chalkboard and have each student copy the list for his or her own use. Encourage spontaneous brainstorming, and do not ask participants to justify their choices. Continue as long as time allows or until students have no more ideas. The final list should contain a wide variety of perceptions. Some of the words will be objectively visual in nature, such as *blue* or *pattern* or *apple;* others will be extremely subjective in nature, such as *happy, evil,* or *king.* A little guidance might be necessary to elicit as broad a range of words as possible, but these spontaneous responses to works of art can be very illuminating.

Instructional tip: For young children, you could make a master list that stays on the board or pass out a copy of the list to all students at a later time.

---

4. It is beneficial, if time allows, to discuss what the word list reveals about the work of art, or at least some of the implications.

5. Engage the students in a more structured exploration of the intrinsic qualities of the work (what the viewer can know strictly by looking at the piece). Focus first on those aspects that are unarguable, such as colors, shapes, or type of balance. Encourage the class to explore the objective content first, so that nothing is missed. Then gradually move into speculation or interpretation. For instance, "I see a man wearing a crown" is a statement of fact (unless the work is extremely abstract), whereas "I see a king" is an interpretation, unless the word *king* appears in the work. Then the students may start inferring meaning from the piece, or even decide that it *has* no meaning.

6. The next part of the process involves learning extrinsic information (information gleaned from research) about the artwork. Biographical information about the artist, prior discussion or criticism of the work, its place in history, the name of the artist if the work is unsigned, and when it was created if it is undated are forms of extrinsic information. (For more on this aspect of art criticism, see The Blue Pot Culture lesson on page 54.) This step can be done in any of several ways, depending upon the time available and the age of the students:

   - In my class, I hand out a packet of information about the artist and his or her works and ask the students to familiarize themselves with the contents before the next class.

- Another possibility would be to have the pupils read the material together in class, or break the material and students into groups, making each group responsible for a different portion of the packet.

- For young children or when time is short, you could present the key concepts to the class yourself.

- Conversely, if you want to stress research skills, you could simply give the students the artist's name and have them use the library or Internet to obtain information.

Instructional tip: During the discussion of intrinsic qualities, the students will probably make certain assumptions or produce certain interpretations of the piece. Study of extrinsic information can reinforce these ideas, expand them, or alter them entirely. Depending on what you wish to achieve through the poetry-writing segment, you may choose to defer the use of extrinsic material until after the writing is completed, leave it up to the student, or eliminate this step altogether. You may also wish to spend some time discussing various types of poetry, such as sonnets, epic poetry, blank verse, free verse, haiku, rhyme schemes, and so on. Language arts and visual arts teachers could do this as a joint project.

---

7. Using any or all of the information gleaned during the exercise, each student writes a poem about the artwork. The actual lesson may be done in several ways:

   - I assign the poetry writing as an independent project, done on the students' own time in whatever poetic style they choose, but this could be an in-class project as well.

   - Since the class has already generated a word list and discussed this particular piece of art, students have a head start on vocabulary and interpretation. You may wish to read poetry created by previous students about that piece, then have the class create a collaborative poem about it.

   - Currently I allow each student to select a different work to write about as their independent project. I have each student turn in a small reproduction of the chosen work (a postcard, Internet print, or photocopy) with his or her poem, and I display the poem and artwork together. I require that the final poem be clear and legible, preferably word processed on a computer. I allow students to embellish the poem with decorations if they wish.

Instructional tip: Have each student turn in a rough draft in advance of the final due date, so that you can catch errors or problems.

Variations

I believe it is helpful for most students to do the first parts of this project as a group, but after they have had some experience in generating word lists and interpretations, there is no reason why they could not select their own artifacts and work independently. Indeed, students with good verbal and interpretive skills might prefer this approach.

When I do this project, I have a variety of curricular reasons for leaving the assignment as open-ended as possible. If I were to include it in a different part of my program, however, I might alter it in a number of ways. To incorporate this project into art history, I would select a piece from the culture or era under discussion and assign an appropriate poetic form as well. Thus, students might write haiku in response to a *sumi-e* scroll or a sonnet to accompany a painting by English Renaissance court painters. If I were addressing elements and principles of art, I could base the poetry assignment on elements or principles of poetry, or focus on a particular feature such as color or texture or value. Most probably I would relate the assignment to the study of rhythm, a principle common to both art and poetry. You need only use your imagination.

FICTION WRITING

A similar process as that outlined in the previous lesson can be used to help students generate works of fiction. You will want to select artwork that is appropriate to the type of fiction you wish students to generate, such as a satire, fable, mystery, fairy tale, or legend. Here are a few options for writing assignments:

Word lists: The word list concept could be enlarged to include brief phrases, or you could guide the class in a particular direction. That is, you might ask for words or phrases that have application only to the setting or to a particular character. Or perhaps you could focus on responses that reflect mood.

Constructing stories around artwork: You might pick a small piece of sculpture or pottery and instruct the students to have the work play a central role in a story—sort of a *Maltese Falcon* approach.

More stories: You might assign each student the same artifact but in a different time period. You could start with the premise that the subject has been passed down from generation to generation, and then have the class weave the resulting stories together into a single narrative. It might be fun to have the students figure out how to link the segments. For example, how did the artwork that was in England during the last story segment suddenly show up in Thailand? Certainly some research would have to be done on the origin of the piece, and the class might well discuss its intrinsic and extrinsic qualities. Students would each be required to describe the work in detail in the course of their writing. It might be very illuminating to see how these descriptions vary, depending upon the point of view of the student (or the character).

Defining plot elements with art: Another approach would be to use a narrative tapestry, painting, sculpture, vase, or similar object to define the setting or characters or mood of the assigned story.

Controversial art: You might choose an extremely provocative piece such as Chris Ofili's *The Holy Virgin Mary,* which depicts the Virgin embellished with elephant dung. You might recall that New York Mayor Rudolph Giuliani moved to cut off city funding to the Brooklyn Museum when the museum included this painting in its *Sensation* show. A visitor to the show spread white paint over the painting, calling it "blasphemy," as museum guards stood by. Students could write a story about a small town's reaction to the selection of a similar piece by the local museum.

Mood stories: Students could write a tale based upon the mood created by a Color-Field painting or, as a Formalist exercise, you might ask them to structure a story in a way they think reflects a recent piece by Frank Stella or Ellsworth Kelly.

Historically concurrent literature and art forms: You might once again select a literary form that is historically concurrent with the artwork, such as a fable for a Roman animal mosaic, a legend for an African mask, a Gothic thriller for an Albert Pinkham Ryder painting, or a stream-of-consciousness tale for a Surrealist or Abstract Expressionist work. Non-art teachers might want to browse an art history text for inspiration. If you are an art teacher trying to encourage writing as well as deep engagement with a work of art, you might choose differently from a creative writing teacher who wants to focus on plot devices or character development. And once again, you might wish to make this an interdepartmental project.

Collaborative science-fiction projects: Perhaps the history or social studies, art, and language arts teachers at your school could do a collaborative unit on the Futurist movement of the early twentieth century. Futurist philosophy, with its glorification of industrial power and mechanical devices, would be a great catalyst for a science-fiction story or perhaps a tale about the dilemma of the individual in a mass society.

Genre tie-ins: If you are working on a particular literary genre in your class—such as works by black authors—you could explore art works by black artists for inspiration.

A corollary to this idea can help students get more from their reading. Simply ask students to illustrate descriptive passages from the text under discussion. Judy Libby, a high-school literature teacher in Indianapolis, uses this device and finds it very productive. This approach can illuminate the writer's setting or help bring a character to life. If students have difficulty drawing, they might be asked to find a painting, drawing, sculpture, or perhaps a work of architecture that they feel is consonant with the author's intent.

It would be particularly interesting to use this approach to compare descriptive qualities in different writing samples. The more evocative the passage, the more easily the reader should be able to illustrate it. It might be especially productive to have creative writing students exchange their writing with classmates for purposes of illustration. They could then judge the success of their efforts by how well the classmate's illustration matches their intent. Or students could illustrate their own work and ask classmates to judge whether or not the art reflects the image they formed from the written word alone.

Book Publishing

A wonderful way to combine art and writing is to have students write children's literature. In our school, pupils in upper grades frequently pair up with "buddies" in lower grades. One of the things the older students do for the younger ones is to write and illustrate a special book, typically featuring that child as a character. Another assignment I give my eighth graders is to create a device for teaching an element or principle of art to a young child, and many choose to make a book for this purpose (see figure 24). The illustrations can be done by hand or on a computer. Of course, students could write and illustrate adult literature, but children's books work well for a variety of reasons. They

Figure 24. Eighth grader Ellen Edenberg created this delightful volume as a device to teach an element of art to a young child.

are shorter by nature, the genre encourages great creativity in solving visual problems, and the wide variety of acceptable styles and materials makes the project somewhat less daunting to the illustrator who has little or no art background.

WRITING AND ILLUSTRATING A CHILDREN'S BOOK

This project could be as simple or elaborate as the participants wish. Commercially marketed blank books for this type of assignment can be ordered from catalogs or purchased at a variety of stores. Or the project could be expanded to incorporate various methods of bookbinding and printing. (The production of limited-edition, handmade books is a surprisingly lucrative aspect of the art scene. These can assume a wide variety of forms and materials.) Students could study the history of books, including the use of papyrus, illuminated manuscripts, and the invention of the printing press. The economics of publishing, or a field trip to a bookstore or printer, might be incorporated. Perhaps an illustrator or author might visit the class.

Procedure

1. Bring in a large number of children's books for the class to look at. Discuss fonts, layout, paper quality, artistic styles, color—in short, anything and everything that might contribute to the final product.

2. You may have a specific theme in mind for the story: biographies or legends, for example, or perhaps the nature of good plot on a simple level. Art teachers might use such a project to reinforce the elements or principles of art or the art of other cultures. In fact, science, social studies, a foreign language, or virtually any other subject matter could be incorporated into the text.

3. Once the story has been written, you must decide how it will be printed and illustrated. Using materials as basic as copier paper (lightly lined if necessary), the students might simply write the story by hand, leaving blank spaces or pages for drawings. The book could be bound by stapling or sewing. At the other end of the spectrum, the authors might create their texts and illustrations on a computer and have the product bound at a print shop. Pages may be laminated and many schools have machines that put plastic spines on texts. In a more advanced

art class, the students might print the pages using lithography or silk screen. Or perhaps your school has industrial arts classes that would like to be involved in the process.

Instructional tip: If you use the commercially available blank books, I strongly urge you to have students place a piece of lined paper under each sheet for neatness. Have students print carefully with a pencil. Check the pencil stage for borders and adequate space for illustrations, then have students write over the pencilled words with a pen that does not smear. Illustrations should be *tipped in;* that is, drawn on separate pieces of paper and pasted into the book.

---

4. Deciding which scenes of the story should be illustrated can lead to some very productive discussions. Be sure to have students make these decisions in time to alter the text, because they may lead to rewriting or expanding descriptive passages.

5. The illustrations themselves can be in any form you or the students desire. You could even have students create pop-up books. There are several instructional manuals on this technique, and some of the processes are relatively simple.

Instructional tip: If an illustrator wishes to use artwork other than drawings or photographs—such as sculpture, collages, or a montage—the object can simply be photographed and the photos inserted in the volume. If you have access to a computer with a scanner and color printer, simply scan in the photograph or actual artwork and use the print in the final book. Color copiers are another, albeit pricey, way to produce flat copies or multiples. (Black-and-white copiers actually can produce some outstanding effects, and colored paper can be used for pizzazz.)

Variations

Developing a story around art: Art students or young children could be asked to draw a picture of anything they wished—as fancifully or as realistically as they desire. Then they or other students could be assigned the task of developing a story to go with the picture (having students write about each other's art is an interesting way to explore how everyone interprets a piece of art differently).

Comic books: Comic books offer another avenue to explore, one which might engage otherwise apathetic students. In this vein, you might introduce older students to the *Maus* graphic novels by Art Speigelman. These Holocaust-related tales would be an excellent vehicle for integrating art, literature, and history.

Autobiography

Lesson Summary

Students examine a portrait or sculpture, then make up answers to a list of biographical questions about the person depicted. Using this information, they write an imaginary "autobiography," in which they pretend to be the person in the artwork.

Purpose

To engage students of all ages in the act of viewing portraiture; to focus on the qualities inherent in good portraiture; to inspire the development of a character or an entire short story.

Materials

❑ one artwork for the class or a different piece for each student (teacher-assigned or student-selected)

❑ list of questions (see step 3)

❑ writing paper and pens

AUTOBIOGRAPHY

Autobiography is a lesson that works equally well for an art specialist, a drama instructor, or a teacher who is looking for a concept to inspire creative writing. It is a good exercise for character development or to generate a story.

Procedure

1. This lesson could be presented in a variety of ways. You might have each participant work from a different portrait (either painted or sculpted), if enough are available (art postcards work well in a classroom setting). Ideally, each student should be allowed to choose a piece that engages him or her. Perhaps you might purposely have more than one student work from the same piece to show how art may be interpreted differently by different viewers.

2. Instruct students not to look at any information about the portrait, such as the title, artist's name, or date of completion. Their impressions should be based entirely upon the visual information intrinsic to the artwork.

3. Provide a list of questions that students are to answer as if they were the person in the portrait or sculpture. The following questions are suggested by the Indianapolis Museum of Art. Use these to inspire your own list:

   - What is your name?

   - How old are you?

   - In what year were you born?

   - Where were you born, and where do you live at the time this portrait was completed?

   - What do you do for a living?

   - What is your hobby?

   - What is your favorite food? Book? Music?

   - What do you do for fun?

   - What advice did your mother always give you?

- What one thing would you never, ever do?
- What one thing would you say to the people of today?

Here are other questions I have added:

- What secret have you never told anyone?
- What are you most afraid of?
- What are you proudest of?
- Whom do you admire the most?
- Who are your friends?

4. Students use the information they invent about the person in the portrait to create an autobiographical work. They could write an essay or biographical fiction, give an oral presentation, or even assume the role of the person in the portrait and give a monologue, with appropriate accents and demeanor.

Instructional tip: I first performed this exercise orally with a group of art teachers, and the results were not only illuminating, but frequently hilarious. Even self-identified "shy" people had great success with their presentations. I have never looked at a portrait in quite the same way since. I currently use this exercise as an addendum to our unit on Baroque art. As the final project for this unit, the students create full-length portraits of themselves as they might have appeared during the Baroque or Rococo era (see the Self-Portrait lesson on page 90). When the painting is complete, I ask each pupil to turn in a one-page response to the questions, which is then hung above his or her "self-portrait." Another project combining a self-portrait and autobiographical materials is depicted in figure 25.

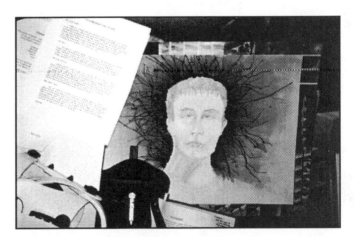

Figure 25. Eighth-Grade Extravaganza was conceived by Mary Ann Yedinak and is sponsored by the Language Arts Department. Students create exhibits about themselves incorporating auto-biographical information, both written and visual. Here, Matt Yacko presents a powerful self-portrait in words and drawing.

Journaling

One of the most interesting ways to inspire writing through art is in the form of journaling. Most literature teachers are familiar with "reader's response" notebooks, and many art teachers have students work on sketch diaries outside of class. You might consider using works of art or art-related topics, such as aesthetics and criticism, as starting points for assignments. I referred to this possibility briefly in the Creative Writing lessons (see pages 99–105).

I start almost every week of the school year by handing each eighth grader a slip of paper with a quotation or question on it. The student glues this into his or her journal and jots down whatever thoughts the quotation inspires. I have included several of my choices among the chapter epigraphs in this book. I am frequently impressed by the perceptive comments I find in my students' journals.

Such notebooks are also a great place to keep cartoons. Of course I encourage my students to clip out pertinent articles for their journals and to jot down visual or conceptual ideas in them, but cartoons and humor are an often-overlooked measure of artistic literacy. In order to "get" a cartoon or joke about art, you must have some familiarity with the concept or work being lampooned. *Calvin and Hobbes* by Bill Watterson was a wonderful source for extremely perceptive comments on the nature of contemporary art.

Symbolism

As discussed in part 1, symbolism is a device common to many disciplines and certainly to literature and art (see figure 26). Because many students learn visually, exploring the symbols used in a work of art may help language arts students understand the concept of symbolism as it applies to literature. Symbolism in art could certainly be used to reinforce the imagery used in a particular historical era and to aid pupils in relating to the culture under discussion.

THE ARNOLFINI MARRIAGE

A great example of the use of symbolism in art is the painting by Jan van Eyck entitled *The Arnolfini Marriage*. The picture presents full-length portraits of Arnolfini and his bride. They stand very symmetrically in a sumptuous bedroom, complete with Oriental rugs, a four-poster bed with red velvet hangings, a fine brass chandelier, a chest, and a convex mirror that fills the wall between them. Arnolfini, dressed in luxurious brown garments and stockinged feet, stands to the viewer's left. At the far left of the canvas is a window, with an orange on the sill. Arnolfini holds his bride's right hand in his left one. She gathers huge folds of the rich, green fabric of her gown in her left hand, which rests on her abdomen. A small dog stands between them, and we can see two pairs of shoes on the floor.

Figure 26. As a seventh grader, Jenny Kruger used discarded shoes as a powerful symbol in her poignant response to a Holocaust-related history assignment.

Everything in this picture is symbolic. The picture itself is a wedding contract, proof of the event. If we look closely at the convex mirror on the back wall, we see not only the rear view of the couple, as we would expect, but we also see the reflection of two people entering a door that faces the mirror. These two figures represent the artist and another witness to the rite. Indeed, the artist's signature and date are boldly inscribed just above the mirror. Translated, the inscription reads "Jan van Eyck was here in 1434." The rest of the imagery attests to the wealth, piety, and (hoped-for) fertility of the union. In the symbolism of the time, the dog represents fidelity; the orange on the windowsill, known also as Adam's apple, refers to forbidden fruit (lust); and the fact that the couple have removed their shoes implies the holy nature of the ground upon which they stand—the sanctity of marriage. The crystal rosary beads hanging next to the mirror were a typical engagement present from a man to his prospective bride: the rosary symbolizing the wife's duty to remain devout and the crystal representing purity. The mirror is surrounded with illustrations of the fourteen stations of the cross, and the chandelier contains only one candle, representing the oneness of God. The wealth of the merchant is reflected in the imported rugs, the expensive furs and velvets, and the presence on the cabinet of more oranges, an extremely costly delicacy. Hanging on the bedpost is a whisk broom, a housewife's attribute, and sitting on top of the post is a small figure symbolic of fertility. The draping of the bride's skirt mimics pregnancy, another image of fertility. (Records reveal that the couple never had children.) Contemporary viewers would easily have understood the meanings encoded in the painting.

VANITAS PAINTINGS

Another rich source of symbols may be found in the exquisite still-life paintings that emerged in Holland during the 1600s. Like the Arnolfini portrait, these pieces can certainly stand on their own visually, but they are far more fascinating if one understands the nature of *vanitas* paintings. These works are actually cautionary morality pieces, reminding the rich patron that earthly wealth is fleeting and that one must attend to his or her soul. Each flower, fruit, knife, or compote tells a story to those who understand the "language." Here are some of the more common symbols:

The cycle of life: There are allusions to the cycle of life—birth, life, and death. In the case of flowers, for instance, you will find blossoms in different stages of maturity, from buds to perfect blooms to overblown or wilting petals, all sharing the same canvas. In the case of fruit, you will find green, fully ripened, and rotting or partly eaten examples simultaneously represented.

Floral symbols: Different flowers have their own individual symbolism. The lily, for example, represents purity as well as the Virgin Mary. Other flowers may stand for passion, sacrifice, and so on.

Symbols of wealth: Bouquets may be comprised of expensive blooms that would never have been available at the same time of year, thus representing the great wealth of the painting's owner. Similarly, silver and crystal goblets and utensils reflect wealth, as do exotic fruits and vegetables.

Bread: Wheat may symbolize bread, which is not only the staff of life but the body of Christ, just as wine stands for his blood.

Time: Items such as hourglasses and globes refer to the passage of time.

Insects: Butterflies allude to the metamorphosis of the soul. Snails and caterpillars are lowly creatures that crawl upon the earth.

Suggested Resource

Chinese and Japanese art offer wonderful opportunities for the study of symbolism in non-Western art. Native American pieces, pre-Columbian artifacts, Hindu, Buddhist, Islamic, and African objects are rich sources as well. Indeed, one might explore symbols that are specific to particular cultures and compare the ways in which they are used in visual and literary arts.

Foreign Languages

Teachers of foreign languages are in a great position to introduce students to the visual arts produced by different cultures. Just as students are eventually exposed to great literature in various languages, so too might they become familiar with great art. At Sycamore, where all the students study Spanish, the rooms used for that purpose are filled with visual aids. Among these are posters of pre-Columbian works, reproductions of paintings by famous artists from Spanish-speaking countries, and even small examples of folk art. Students are assigned essays, research papers, and oral presentations about visual artists, and the symbolism used in various countries is discussed. Certainly foreign language teachers who work with young children use visuals to reinforce verbal skills and memory, and it would not be hard to include fine arts in such lessons.

PROJECT IDEAS

Most of the suggestions outlined previously in this chapter could be adapted by foreign language teachers to improve students' performance in their subject and expand their knowledge of art as well. Here are a few other ideas:

Foreign-language museum tours: At North Central High School in Indianapolis, certain upper-level language classes have visited the Indianapolis Museum of Art for tours of pertinent works conducted in the language being studied.

Art videos: Perhaps you could find a video about an artist of your culture, either in English or in the language you are teaching. Likewise, art teachers can reinforce their students' language studies by presenting works by appropriate artists in their classes.

> *"I believe art is a good way to express feelings and ideas. It encourages analytical thinking when creating or judging the piece. I also love the creativity involved in it. Secondly, I think art can give a little boost to someone's self-esteem. Knowing that you can create these wonderful things . . . gives you a sense of accomplishment."*
>
> —Lauren, Sycamore student

Researching artists of the culture: As suggested in part 1, you could have students research various artists who speak the language you teach, select their favorite, and explain in that language why they chose that artist.

Writing as art: In some cultures, such as Chinese and Japanese, language and art are very closely associated. In many cases, the written form of the language actually *is* art, so teachers of these subjects have an even greater opportunity to focus on the relationship of these two disciplines. ❧

CHAPTER 11
Science

"The most beautiful thing we can experience is the mysterious.
It is the true source of all art and science."

—Albert Einstein

Many people think of science and art as occupying opposite ends of a methodological spectrum, where art is perceived to be the product of pure creativity and science is the child of factual data and research. In reality, however, the two are far more similar in procedure than one might guess, and both disciplines share a heavy reliance on technology and discovery (see figure 27).

Suggested Resources

Visual aids can take a variety of forms:

- Take 5 Art Prints has a series called *Art and Science: Natural Environments* (available through several of the catalogs listed in the References and Resources).

- You might display reproductions of the works of John James Audubon or selections from Leonardo da Vinci's diaries.

- You can purchase mobiles or hang prints of works by mobile creator Alexander Calder.

- For paintings with scientific content, you might explore Joseph Wright's *The Experiment with an Air Pump,* Rembrandt van Rijn's *Dr. Tulp's Anatomy Lesson,* or Thomas Eakins's *The Gross Clinic* or *The Agnew Clinic.* Michelangelo also incorporated biological information in his works, as I describe on page 128.

- You could choose Impressionist pieces to spark discussions about the physics of light or Cubist works to show one way that artists dealt with questions of spatial and temporal reality.

Figure 27. Jared Spaans expressed his love of science in his self-portrait for the Eighth-Grade Extravaganza. He used discarded computer parts, among other things, for this figure. A battery and switch allow the eyes to light up.

The Physics of Light

Lesson Summary

Students identify colors in a lighted room, then identify what they see in a completely dark room. They observe how white light is broken into its component colors by a prism, then discuss how we perceive various hues.

Purpose

To understand that color is a function of light; to understand that black is the absence of light; to observe how white light is broken into a spectrum of colors; to understand how we perceive colors; to define *pigment*.

Materials

- ❑ A storage room or closet without windows that will hold several people
- ❑ a prism or similar device
- ❑ white and black objects

Suggested Resource

A wonderful resource for art and science teachers alike is Leonard Shlain's fascinating book *Art and Physics: Parallel Visions in Space, Time, and Light*. Although you may not agree with all of his interpretations, the scope of the work and his overall thesis are thought-provoking and offer exciting ways to link artistic and scientific theory.

The Science of Light

Since color is a quality of light, understanding light is integral to visual arts. I begin by introducing the concept that color is light. Then we explore mixing primary colors to create secondaries (colors comprised of equal parts of two primary colors). We also explore complementary colors and how the human visual system encodes images.

THE PHYSICS OF LIGHT

At Sycamore, art students are introduced to the science of light in the first grade, so the following lesson is geared to early elementary students. With some modifications, the following techniques could be adapted to older students who have never studied this area.

Materials tip: For a prism, I prefer the plastic eyeglasses that fracture light into a spectrum when you look through them. These can be bought at certain stores and museums, and sometimes from catalogs.

Procedure

1. With the lights on, ask the students to look around the room and tell you where the color is. Most will point to the pictures on the walls, bulletin boards, clothing, construction paper—whatever seems colorful to them. Some will say that the color is "everywhere."

2. Take the class to a room that can be completely darkened. Point out all the colors, then turn the lights off briefly. Have students describe what they see, trying to elicit the word *black,* not just *dark.*

3. Return to the classroom and once again ask the students where the color is. Most will realize by now that the color is in the light. Because the color is in the light, and black is what you get when you take away the light, then you have also shown that black is not a color, it is the absence of light.

4. Once you have shown that one must have light in order to have color in general, you are ready to discuss the reason we see particular colors. Explain that the light we get from our sun is called *white light* and that it contains all of the colors in the rainbow mixed together.

5. Set up your prism or hand out the plastic glasses and show the students the phenomenon of rainbows created when white light is passed through something that breaks it into its component parts. I explain that different colors of light have different wavelengths and speeds, so each one passes through the material differently. This is also a great time to discuss why we sometimes see rainbows in the sky. Reiterate that when all the colors of light mix together, they result in a perfectly clear light that we call "white." (I will explain why it is white later in the lesson.)

Instructional tip: Some of you may be familiar with the spinning tops that come with interchangeable disks of various colors. These are frequently sold in museum shops or science stores. When you spin certain colors fast enough, they will create white, which is another nice demonstration to include in this lesson.

---

6. Ask students, "When all the colors in your paint box are mixed together, do they make white?" Most children have already experienced that when they mix all their paints or markers or crayons, they get a brownish-gray mush. If not, you might do a demonstration in the front of the room or have each child mix crayon or chalk or paint colors at their seats. They will quickly see that when pigments are blended together, they do not make white or clear.

Instructional tip: Since we have already discussed primary colors by this time, I also explain that the primary colors of light are red, green, and blue rather than red, yellow, and blue. Primary colors are important for two reasons: they can be mixed to create all the other colors, yet no other colors can be mixed to form a primary.

---

7. Conclude that pigments are different from light. *Pigment* is a substance which causes light to be absorbed or reflected in ways that result in the appearance of color.

8. Find a student who is wearing a pure color, such as red. Stand behind the child and ask the class why the piece of clothing looks red. After eliciting a few ideas, I give an explanation like the following (this example assumes the child is wearing red):

    > Janey's shirt is having a party, and all the colors want to come, but in order to get in, they have to be invited in. All the colors of the rainbow are in the white light that is hitting the shirt. The yellow light knocks on the shirt (here I "knock" on the student's shoulder) and asks, "May I come in?" and the shirt says, "Sure! You are very welcome!" Then the green light knocks, asking, "May I come to the party?" . . . "Sure, come right on in!" (Repeat this for orange, blue, and violet). Then the red light knocks on the shirt and asks, "May I come to the party?" And the shirt says, "No! We are completely full, and there is no room for any more light." For some reason, the *pigment* in this shirt will not allow red light in. The red light has to go somewhere, so it bounces off the shirt and hits my eye. The sensation travels up my optic nerve to my brain. If you were born in the United States, you probably learned to call this sensation *red*. What would you call it if you were born in Mexico? (*Rojo.*) Does anyone know what you would call this sensation in France? What about in China? (Obviously, the greater the ethnic mix in your class, the more color words you can elicit.)

    Instructional tip: You certainly could come up with many other ways to conceptualize this phenomenon—such as magic keys, special doorways, or passwords. Several years ago a first grader suggested the party scenario, and the other students just loved the image. I find that when we review this concept in second grade, the "party" image has really stuck!

    ---

9. After the explanation of a single color, I find something black in the room, and I ask the students who is coming to *this* party. (If a student guesses that the black light could not "get in," I ask whether there is black in a rainbow.) Most students will guess "all of the light" or "none of it." Remind the class of their experience in the dark room. What caused the sensation of black? It occurred when *no light* hit their eyes. If no light is bouncing off to hit their eyes, then *all* the colors must be at the party. Explain that there are two reasons why the eye might

perceive black. Either there is no light source at all, as happened in the dark room, or all (or most) of the light is being absorbed by an object.

10. Turn to something in the room that is white or hold up a piece of paper and ask who is attending *this* party. Elicit that when "normal" light hits an object and *none* of it is allowed in, it *all* bounces back and hits our eye at once. Thus, when all the light mixed together bounces off something, we perceive that object as white. If such light simply hits our eye without bouncing off of something, it appears to be clear.

Variations

Pigment: Several nice lessons can be introduced on the concept of *pigment*. You might discuss the pigment *chlorophyll*—which will not let green light in—and how it leaves some trees in the fall, allowing us to see the "true" colors of the trees. You could also discuss *melanin,* the pigment in skin, and why two people can have very different skin tones even though all humans share the same pigmentation (another opportunity to reinforce affective education about tolerance). *Protective coloration,* the concept that animals' coats are patterned and colored to help them camouflage themselves in their environments, could form the basis of another lesson.

Value: Because my subject is art, I introduce the concept of *value.* For artists, black and white are not colors; they are values. *Value* refers to how the artist uses light and dark. White is the lightest light and black is the darkest dark (although now that artists are using actual light in installations and Conceptual pieces, it is possible to have an intense wattage that might be considered lighter than white). Each color has value, and there are also a huge variety of grays.

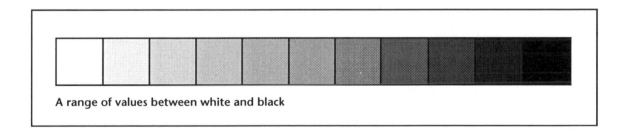

A range of values between white and black

Light and heat: This might be a great time to relate light to heat. We usually discuss why white clothing is cooler than black clothing, or why you might choose different values for roofs in different climates.

Qualities of Light

Lesson Summary

We have seen that we perceive color based upon the type of light that bounces off an object. Imagine that an object contains a pigment that makes it appear red. That is, when light hits it, only the red light bounces off and hits your eye. But what happens if the light you shine on the object has no red in it or a slightly different kind of red? There is a simple and enjoyable way to find out.

Purpose

To observe how the color of a light source changes the colors we perceive.

Materials

- ❑ a contained light source (e.g., a powerful flashlight or a slide or filmstrip projector)
- ❑ colored gels, overhead projector film, or plastic report covers
- ❑ projector screen or other white surface for reflecting light

QUALITIES OF LIGHT

Once you have established that color is actually a function of light, you can introduce an important corollary: the quality of the light affects what color we perceive. Not all light is white. Neon bulbs give off a different sort of light than incandescent ones, and neither is exactly the same as sunlight, although there are new bulbs on the market that are designed to come extremely close. This is a particularly important concept, not only for artists but for people trying to match colors for any reason. I introduce this exercise in second grade and repeat it for new students in third, and the children absolutely love it.

Procedure

1. Pull down your projector screen (or tape a piece of white paper on the chalkboard) and darken the room as much as possible.

2. Turn on the projector or flashlight, aim it onto the screen, and ask the students to describe what they see. They will respond "white."

3. Hold a colored gel such as red or blue in front of the light source and ask the same question. Students will perceive that the color of the screen has changed.

4. Find a student with a colorful shirt or dress and ask him or her to stand in front of the screen. Look at the shirt in the normal projector light. Then put a red gel in front of the light. Depending on the colors in the clothing, you should see some drastic changes. Try a green gel, and you should get similarly dramatic results.

Instructional tip: If you understand opposite, or *complementary,* colors (see the next lesson), you can predetermine just how dramatic the change will be. Green light contains no red, and red light contains no green. Thus, if the student's shirt has reds in it, those reds will "glow" under a red gel, but they will turn black under a green one. Yellows will seem to disappear against a white background. You might want to experiment beforehand to insure the best results in class.

---

5. Talk about how important it is to match colors in the type of light under which they will be viewed. Ask how many students have had the experience of choosing colors under store lights, only to find that in the sunlight or lamplight the colors no longer match. You can mention how such practical considerations are important in careers such as interior decoration or clothing design and that even fine artists need to consider the kind of light in which their work will viewed. The same holds true in scientific areas in which subtle color differences are important. For example, a doctor might fail to notice an unhealthy hue to the skin under the wrong kind of light!

COMPLEMENTARY COLORS

The following exercise can be used with even the youngest students. With minor adjustments, it can be used for any grade level.

Suggested Resource

Depending on the age of your students, you might want to show them the delightful Eric Carle book *Hello, Red Fox,* which demonstrates the phenomenon of complementary colors.

Procedure

1. Introduce the subject of opposites. Ask the students to name the opposite of several common words. Finish the list with *black* or *white,* then ask what the opposite of *red* is. Students will make a variety of guesses.

2. Explain that just as black and white are opposites, each color has an opposite of its own, and that opposites behave in very special ways.

3. Show several examples of black-and-white designs that vibrate or result in ghost images if stared at. Discuss *afterimages* briefly: The brain takes little pictures of things we stare at and holds them for a very brief time. Ask students whether they have ever

Complementary Colors
Lesson Summary
Students stare closely at different colored shapes against a white background. When the shape is removed, they see an afterimage of that color's complement. They predict which colors are opposites.

Purpose
To introduce the concepts of *complementary,* or opposite, colors; afterimages; and rods and cones.

Materials
- [ ] black-and-white optical illusions that cause ghost images
- [ ] offprints of art by Bridget Riley (optional)
- [ ] photographic negatives
- [ ] 6"–8" shapes cut from colored acetate (e.g., overhead projector material), in magenta (cool red), cyan (warm blue), and yellow (if unavailable, you may paint a shape or use construction paper)
- [ ] a large white background (e.g., a projector screen)
- [ ] designs to test for color blindness (optional)

seen the bright TV screen for a few seconds after they have turned it off. Or perhaps they have retained the image of a light bulb after it is no longer lit. Explain that these are afterimages. It is our ability to retain afterimages that allows us to watch movies and cartoons. If our brain did not retain a brief visual memory of each movie frame as it went by, we would see a pretty jerky show!

4. Pass around photographic negatives (a strip of negatives comes with developed photos). Ask how the images on them differ from real, or *positive,* images, eliciting that the light areas are dark and vice versa.

5. Explain that if we stare at an object for a long time, our brain will take a picture as a negative, just like a camera—that is, the lights are dark, the darks are light, and each color is retained as its opposite. (If you have access to software such as Print Shop, you could use it to "reverse" a color picture as a demonstration.)

6. Explain that our eyes have receptor cells called *rods* and *cones.* Rods receive sensations of light and dark, and cones receive sensations of color. Add that we can "overwork" these cells. Ask whether students have ever come into a normally lit building from extremely bright sunlight or entered a darkened movie theater from a well-lit lobby. What happens? The dark seems more intense because it takes your rods a few seconds to adjust. A similar thing happens when we overwork the cones by looking at a particular color for an extended period.

7. Explain that we can use these facts—that the brain holds a brief impression of an image, and that with overwork, the impression becomes a negative, or opposite, of the original—to find the opposite of any color we want.

8. Set up a projector screen or other large white background and hold one of the acetate shapes firmly against it. I usually start with magenta. Ask the students to stare at the shape for about 30 seconds. They may blink occasionally, but it is important for them to keep their eyes focused on the center of the shape. Explain that when the 30 seconds are up, you are going to pull the shape away and they must keep their eyes focused on the white background until the afterimage forms. This may take a couple of seconds, but you will know when they see it, because their faces will simply light up. Ask them what color they see. If you held up a magenta (a cool or pinkish red) shape, the afterimage should appear green.

Instructional tip: If a student does not see anything, it is probably because his or her eyes wandered at some point, but it could imply a color perception problem. You might want to have a book with the designs used to test color blindness handy. (These can be obtained at the library.) Or refer the student to the school nurse or other appropriate personnel to be tested for color blindness.

---

9. Ask the class to tell you the opposite of red. They will now say "green." Ask them the opposite of green. Most will realize that opposites work both ways, but it is a good idea to reinforce the concept with a demonstration. You could simply do this with green acetate, or you could incorporate a demonstration of how primary colors combine to create secondary colors (colors made by mixing equal amounts of two primary colors), as follows:

10. Hold the magenta acetate in one hand and the other two primaries in the other. Explain that even though you do not have a green shape to stare at, you do have blue and yellow ones. Place the blue and the yellow over each other to form a green shape (be sure that all your shapes are identical so that there is no edge of another color showing). Repeat the process of staring at the shape. When you pull the green shape away, the students should see a magenta afterimage. (If you are using painted colors, you could mix paints.)

11. You can then do the same exercise using the blue acetate, which should result in an orange afterimage. Since you have no orange acetate, you will once again have to make it by mixing the other two primaries (that is, red and yellow).

12. Finally, hold up the yellow shape and have students stare at it. The violet afterimage thus created is my favorite, which is why I save it for last. Make purple by overlapping the magenta and blue pieces of acetate and prove the converse by staring. By now, many of my students will be able to predict that the opposite of yellow will be purple, either because it is the only secondary left or because they have reasoned out that the opposite of each primary color is the secondary color you get when you mix the other two primaries.

Instructional tip: If you have a color wheel in your room, now is a great time to point out that opposite colors lie directly across from—or opposite—each other on the wheel.

Applications of Complementary Colors

Lesson Summary

Students stare at sheets of red and green construction paper placed next to each other to observe a brightening effect of the colors. They may experiment with mixing complementary colors to create a duller or grayer intensity of the original color.

Purpose

To understand how complementary colors affect each other; to understand the concept of *simultaneous contrast.*

Materials

- ❑ sheets of red and green construction paper
- ❑ books or art prints of black-and-white designs that create optical illusions of "vibrating" or "jumping" when you look at them
- ❑ crayons or paints in complementary colors
- ❑ white painting or drawing paper

13. Explain that artists call opposite colors *complementary.* I like to point out the difference between a *complement* and a *compliment* and to discuss the root of the word *complete.* Any two complementary colors actually contain all three primaries in some proportion, so in a sense you have a "complete" color wheel. You may also remind the students that because pigment and light have different primaries, the complements will be different as well.

APPLICATIONS OF COMPLEMENTARY COLORS

For a further art tie-in, you may discuss why it is very important for artists to know the opposite of each color and to understand how complementary colors behave. This concept has practical applications in other fields as well.

Suggested Resources

- You might explore the works of Bridget Riley, a famous British Op artist, as well as books of moiré designs and optical illusions.
- Many science centers have hands-on demonstrations of the effects of complementary colors, and this might be a good field trip for a science class

Procedure

When complementary colors are placed next to each other, both colors seem much brighter. They may almost glow or may seem to vibrate. You can demonstrate how this happens as follows:

1. Ask the students what they noticed while staring at the colored shapes. Did anything happen around the outside of the shape? Long before you pulled the shape away, they probably noticed that a "halo" of the opposite color formed around it.

2. Explain that every color we look at is accompanied by a halo of its opposite, but we do not usually notice it. This halo has an effect upon the color next

to it, however, and this effect is known as *simultaneous contrast*. In the case of complements, the halo serves to brighten the neighboring color. If you place a red shape next to a green shape, the red shape will "cast" a green light all around itself. Where the green halo falls on the green shape, it will have the effect of increasing the amount of green light that is hitting your eye. The same will be true of the green shape's red halo as it crosses the red shape.

3. To demonstrate this effect, hold a piece of red construction paper right next to a piece of green. Ask the students to stare at the line where the two overlap. After several seconds, ask what they are perceiving. They will see the line start to vibrate, and they might even see it turn white or black before a strip brightens on both sides of it.

4. Explain that artists use this effect in a variety of ways from grabbing our attention in an ad to selecting fabrics and wallpapers. You might show black-and-white designs that appear to "jump" when stared at. (No one is sure why this effect occurs. It could be the result of rods being "overworked" or it could be that the brain is confused about which is the background, the black or the white.)

When complementary colors are *mixed*, on the other hand, they dull each other. True opposites are the only pairs of colors you can mix without getting a new color. If you mix true opposites equally, you should get gray or black. You can demonstrate this effect using paints or crayons. Reds and greens work best. *Beware*, however, that the materials we are given in school are rarely true colors. The "red" crayon or paint may be a great color, but it is usually not the red that is the opposite of the "green" in the same set. So you may need to play around with violet reds and chartreuses and such to find the true colors or you will get a sort of nasty brownish tone rather than a gray.

If you mix true complements unequally, you will get a grayer version of the color you have more of. That is, if you add a few drops of red paint to a cup of green, you should get a duller green, not a bluer or a yellower green. The result will be a different intensity of green, and perhaps (but not necessarily) a different value, but not a different hue (see page 17 for definitions of these terms).

Application Question

There are several practical applications for knowledge about complementary colors. One question I ask my third graders after our review of opposites is, "Why are many operating room walls painted green?" They all realize right away that it has something to do with the fact that blood is red, but it may take a while for them to put it all together. Can you figure it out? The answer is at the end of this chapter.

Fun with Complements

Lesson Summary

Students draw a simple illustration in colors that are complements to the colors normally associated with those objects. They stare at their illustration then at white paper to see an afterimage in the "correct" colors.

Purpose

To learn about complementary colors; to experience visual afterimages.

Materials

☐ 9" x 12" white paper

☐ pencils

☐ markers (preferred) or crayons

☐ chalkboard, whiteboard, or white easel paper

FUN WITH COMPLEMENTS

Once your students are familiar with the three basic pairs of opposites, you can do an enjoyable hands-on project to reinforce the concept.

Procedure

1. Choose subjects that are strongly associated with a specific color. That is, if I say "sky," the first color that pops into your head is probably blue. (As I explain to my students, even though artists can make their sky any color they want, and we all know that the real sky is not always blue, for this project only we are going to use the most common color we can think of for the subject.) Here are the associations I use for early elementary grades:

Object	Normal Color	Opposite Color
sky	blue	orange
sun	yellow	violet
cloud	white	black
brick house	red	green
grass	green	red
mountains	purple	yellow
roof	black	white
an orange tree	green crown, orange oranges, brown trunk	red crown; blue oranges; light blue, warm blue (e.g., robin's egg, azure) or green-blue for the trunk

2. Write the elements of the picture on the chalkboard (or whiteboard) and ask students what color each would normally be. Write the color next to the element. I also outline the picture on my whiteboard in black marker. (You may also outline in pencil on a large sheet of white paper.)

3. Now for the fun part. Explain that students are going to color each part of the picture in the color that is the *opposite* of the one they would normally use. Ask what color is the opposite of the blue in the sky. When they respond with the correct color, write "orange" next to "sky." Since I have a whiteboard, I actually use an orange marker to do this, then color the sky in my picture orange. Go through the entire list of objects and write the opposite color next to each word in a place that can remain in view for reference as long as the students are doing the project. Also color in your sample drawing accordingly. When you get to the tree trunk, explain that every different brown has its own opposite, but that they are going to treat this brown as a dark orange. Ask them the opposites of *dark* and *orange* (that is, light blue).

Instructional tip: Since I have drawn a precise example on my whiteboard, I explain that for this picture, creativity is not the main point. Therefore, just this once, their projects may look like mine.

---

4. Have each student fold a piece of paper in half widthwise to create two 6″ x 9″ areas. Have them open the paper, and *on one half only* draw a picture lightly in pencil that includes all the aforementioned elements. Students should be careful not to cross the fold line. Stress that all the objects should be as large as possible in the space and should be simple with few details. For example, the oranges are just circles.

5. Instruct students that, using markers, they should color their picture as neatly and solidly as possible in the *opposite* colors from normal, using the technique you just showed them. Ask whether they can guess why they are leaving half of their paper blank. Someone may actually get the idea: After they finish coloring the picture in its "opposite" colors, they are going to stare at the center of the colored half then at the white half until the afterimage forms. In the afterimage, of course, the sky will be blue, the grass green, the sun yellow, and so on. If no one guesses correctly, you can provide some subtle clues.

6. When students finish coloring, have them hold the project at arm's length and count slowly to 30. Then they shift their eyes to the white half to see the afterimage in the correct colors. It is important that students hold their pictures still, so have them rest their arms on their desks. If they do not get a clear afterimage, have them focus on a small part of the picture at a time.

The Brain in the Sistine Chapel Ceiling

Several years ago, an article appeared in our newspaper about a local doctor who claimed that Michelangelo had painted a cross section of a brain on the Sistine Chapel ceiling. It seems that after a day of dissecting brains at work, he had come home to find that his new book on Michelangelo had arrived in the mail. Like most books on the great Renaissance artist, it had a large foldout reproduction of the Sistine Chapel ceiling. When his eyes lit on the famous section depicting God creating Adam, he suddenly realized that the great figure of God in his billowing cape, surrounded by small angels, was actually a cross section of a human brain. In the *Journal of the American Medical Association,* the doctor, Frank Lynn Meshberger, explained his theory in detail. Using overlays and diagrams as well as more philosophical proofs, he made an extremely compelling case for his thesis; but I was persuaded long before I finished reading. When you combine the visual evidence with the knowledge that the artist had said that God's greatest gift to man was his intellect—his brain—well! I could not wait to present the newspaper article to my students. Imagine my delight to discover that Dr. Meshberger was a friend of one of our parents.

> *"One may look at a painting and find his or her spirit inside of it . . . We need programs that express the importance of art and all it symbolizes."*
>
> —Kieran, Sycamore student

In the years since his article appeared, Dr. Meshberger has been kind enough to visit our sixth-grade class—the grade that explores the Renaissance—almost every year. His visits are scheduled through the science department, and he always adds some wonderful insight into the science of art. For example, are you familiar with the *Pietà* in St. Peter's Basilica in Rome? Michelangelo created four of these statues of Mary holding Jesus just after the Crucifixion. The piece in St. Peter's is the earliest of the four and the most horizontal, showing Jesus draped across Mary's lap with one arm and hand hanging down. As in most of Michelangelo's sculptures, you can see each vein standing out clearly. But, Dr. Meshberger points out, Michelangelo did dissections himself and was totally familiar with dead bodies. He would have known that the venous system collapses upon death, and that veins would not appear in such a pronounced manner. Was this Michelangelo's way of saying that Jesus *was not dead?* We also know that dissection was against church law. Was encoding the brain in the ceiling the artist's way of subtly tricking the pope who perpetually harassed him? Only someone who did dissections could know what a cross section of a brain looked like.

Note: Sycamore is an independent school with no church affiliation. We have students from all religious and ethnic backgrounds, and we do not promote one religion over another. However, we could not teach about the Middle Ages or the Renaissance without making significant references to Catholicism or showing church imagery. With some modifications, I taught the same art course at a Jewish day school. Students from every background find Dr. Meshberger's theories fascinating. Of course, when we discuss this subject in art class, I do not insist that Dr. Meshberger is correct. I encourage the students to consider his arguments and form their own opinions. Whatever they conclude, the doctor is an outstanding role model for our students, a scientist who is an artist himself and one who takes art as seriously as medicine.

Physics in Architecture

There are a variety of building techniques that could lead quite naturally into a study of physics. For example, rounded arches and pointed arches distribute stress differently. Physics and art teachers could design a lesson in which students construct models covering a given expanse but using a variety of techniques: arch and vault, groin or cross vaults, post and lintel, dome on squinches or pendentives, geodesic domes, and so on. Cantilevering is another architectural device that has its basis in physics. Sugar cubes or balsa wood make inexpensive building materials for constructing the models. The class could compare the efficiency and cost of the various techniques.

UNDERSTANDING FLYING BUTTRESSES

Do the following exercise to help your students compare the supportive qualities of engaged and flying buttresses.

1. Find a hallway or large room where students can all stand against a wall.

2. Have students stand with their backs against a wall, pressing themselves firmly against it so that their heels, bottoms, shoulders, and head are touching it. Explain that they are now *engaged* buttresses, the kind of support that buildings had in Roman times and which supported the weight of most Romanesque cathedrals.

3. Have them imagine that something is pushing with great force against the other side of the wall. Ask, "How well could you hold up the wall in your current position?"

4. Now have students turn around to face the wall and stand about three feet away from it. Their arms should be raised slightly above their head and extended in front of them (as if in position for playing "London Bridge"). They lean forward until they are pushing against the wall. Explain that they are now *flying* buttresses, and ask if they feel more capable of holding up the wall in this position. Obviously they do (see figure 28 below).

Figure 28. Sycamore students practice being engaged and flying buttresses.

Other Ideas

In addition to these ideas, you may wish to review the chapter on technology in part 1.

Aerodynamics: One area of physics that offers strong possibilities for integration is aerodynamics. Designing and creating paper airplanes or kites can involve problems in design as well as science.

Microscopic views: There are several projects that integrate biological sciences with art. One of the simplest and most interesting is to have the students create works of art based upon the view through a microscope. This could lead into a study of organic shapes, color, value, emphasis, gradation, or any other appropriate element or principle of art, as well as causing the students to focus closely on the specimen.

Drawing plants and animals: Perhaps a trip to the zoo for a zoology field trip or to an arboretum or greenhouse for botany could result in some sketching. As I suggested in part 1, asking students to render a single subject in a variety of ways not only fosters creativity but causes them to look more closely. If they are dissecting, having them do a medical illustration of their work can reinforce both drawing and observational skills.

Drawing models: A former student of mine who attends Interlochen Academy in Michigan recently showed me a terrific idea from her life-drawing class. First, a skeleton, such as you find in many science rooms, was posed and the students were asked to draw the bones. Then a model took the same pose as the skeleton, and the students superimposed their sketches of the model over the original skeleton drawing. In a related approach, the students sketched a model, then looked up the various muscles in a text and drew them in on top. Jenny's interpretations were outstanding, but even a less artistically gifted student would get a lot out of such a project.

Leaf compositions: Leaf collections were a standard lesson when I was in school. A delightful twist on this assignment would be to create designs or figures from the leaves. A charming little booklet entitled *A Leaf Zoo,* by C. V. Herder, gives several ideas for such compositions.

Printmaking: Another project that can help to focus on the various forms of fruits and vegetables is printmaking. Fold several paper towels into a pad and place them in a shallow container such as the polystyrene tray that holds meat from the supermarket. Dampen the paper towel pad and spread some tempera paint over its surface. (Make sure the paint is not lumpy.) Cut up a selection of foods with strong shapes. Items that work well are green peppers cut in half (horizontally or vertically), mushrooms cut in half vertically, onions cut horizontally, apples cut in half vertically, and potatoes. Simply press the item into the paper-towel inkpad and then onto a piece of paper. This is a nice project for young children.

Andy Goldsworthy art: The art of Andy Goldsworthy can be a wonderful catalyst for lessons integrating art and science. Goldsworthy is an artist who uses natural materials such as grass, rocks, sand, and snow in situ to create works of astonishing beauty. Any one of his books should offer numerous ideas. At the very least, his works would make excellent visual aids for the classroom.

The chemistry of art: Chemistry can be a productive subject for integration as well. Teachers of either discipline could explore questions such as why Leonardo da Vinci's *Last Supper* fresco flaked off; the chemical difference between pigments and dyes; and what scientific processes, physical and chemical, are involved in glazing ceramics. ❦

Answer to Application Question

Operating rooms are painted green because staring at a blood-spattered field for any length of time will produce an afterimage of green spots. If the doctors and nurses look up at a green wall, the spots will fade into the paint color, allowing their eyes to rest.

CHAPTER 12
Mathematics

"Mathematics . . . possesses . . . supreme beauty . . .
such as only the greatest art can show."

—Bertrand Russell

Mathematics and art have myriad concepts and considerations in common, from extremely technical concerns to general themes. It is not hard to find books that integrate the two subjects, and many math teachers subscribe to the view that manipulation and visual representation are important steps to a thorough understanding of abstract mathematical concepts. As I pointed out in the introduction, certain mathematical principles, such as the Fibonacci numbers and the geometric figure that results from them, have been used by artists from Egyptian and Greek times to the present day. Certainly, one of the easiest and most productive ways to integrate art and mathematics is to have students create designs based upon mathematical concepts. Another approach is to show how such principles apply to well-known artworks.

Suggested Resources

- Posters of M. C. Escher's works make great room decorations.
- Take 5 Art Prints offers sets of interdisciplinary visual aids including *Art and Mathematics* (available through several of the catalogs listed in the References and Resources).

Paula Jurgonski, one of the terrific math teachers at Sycamore, has introduced me to a number of outstanding sources which I urge you to explore. My two favorites are:

- *Mathematical Footprints: Discovering Mathematical Impressions All Around Us* by Theoni Pappas
- *A Beginner's Guide to Constructing the Universe: The Mathematical Archetypes of Nature, Art, and Science* by Michael S. Schneider

Introducing Geometric Shapes

Lesson Summary

The class begins by defining the properties of geometric shapes, then students trace around a variety of geometric shapes to make designs of their own choosing.

Purpose

To define a shape; to understand the properties of geometric shapes; to experience positive and negative space; to create a design using geometric shapes.

Materials

❑ variety of geometric shapes cut from colored and gray poster board:

- 3 sizes of circles, roughly 1½″ to 3½″ in diameter
- 3 sizes of squares, from 1″ to 3″ across
- various kinds of triangles
- rectangles in a range of sizes
- a few small parallelograms

❑ 9″ x 12″ or 12″ x 18″ white construction paper (using smaller paper requires less time)

❑ pencils

❑ broad-tipped black markers

❑ oil pastels (or crayons or markers)

- The basic text *Discovering Geometry: An Inductive Approach* by Michael Serra has some wonderful art references and ideas for projects.

- *Metamorphosis: A Sourcebook of Mathematical Discovery* by Lorraine Mottershead is another good source of references and projects.

- *The Loom of God: Mathematical Tapestries at the End of Time* by C. A. Pickover is an intriguing volume.

- Paula also recommends *The Hands-On Marvelous Ball Book* by Bradford Hansen-Smith for great geometrical folding projects.

Geometry

As you will recall from part 1, shape is an important element of art. Not all closed figures are geometric, however, and helping students recognize the unique properties of geometric shapes is a natural way to integrate mathematics and art.

INTRODUCING GEOMETRIC SHAPES

In first grade, I introduce units on line, form, and shape with definitions that are mathematically compatible, and we discuss such principles as symmetry and asymmetry. The following exercise is an example of such a focus. It provides an enjoyable way for math teachers to reinforce certain geometric concepts and, with some adjustments, could be used with much older students.

Procedure

1. Place several of each shape on the tables before the students enter, then ask them to guess what element of art (or math) the class is going to study. Virtually everyone will answer "shape."

2. Ask whether anyone can define *shape,* eliciting the features that shapes are *flat,* or *two-dimensional, closed* figures. That is, if I draw a line on the board, the

students recognize that it does not become a shape until I bring the line back to where I started. You may wish to discuss the difference between two-dimensional figures and three-dimensional forms.

3. Ask what all these shapes have in common, besides the fact that they are shapes. Even for gifted students, this is a pretty tough question, and they will give many repetitive answers. If no one guesses the answer in a reasonable amount of time, I ask them to tell me exactly what they see on the tables. They will answer "circles, squares, triangles, rectangles, and parallelograms." I ask, "What have you just told me?" If no one figures out what I am after, I draw a very odd organic shape on the board and ask them what it is. This will almost always result in enlightenment. The shapes on the tables have names! Some shapes have names—and rules—and others do not.

4. Make a list of all the shapes that the students can name—hexagons; octagons; trapezoids; isosceles, equilateral, and right triangles; and so on. Define shapes that have names and rules as *geometric*.

5. Pass out white construction paper. Have students trace the shapes on their papers in pencil. They may simply create a design, or they might build an actual image from the shapes—a house, train, truck, rocket, even a dinosaur or robot. Almost any image is possible if you start with enough variation in the sizes of the shapes. Encourage students to overlap the shapes and to fill the entire page.

6. Point out that students are creating *negative spaces;* that is, those spaces left after you have drawn the positive shapes (see the symmetry lessons, especially pages 141–45).

7. When the sheet is filled, have students trace over the lines with a black marker, preferably a broad-tipped one.

8. Finally, they fill all the shapes with oil pastel, using the medium thickly for a rich, velvety effect. If you do not have oil pastels, students could use heavy, solid crayon, or simply use marker for the whole project. (In this case, either have students eliminate the black lines altogether or put them in last, to avoid smearing.)

Piet Mondrian Creations

Lesson Summary

Students create a design using an overlapping or repeated geometric shape, then use primary colors to create visual balance.

Purpose

To focus on achieving balance.

Materials

- ❏ 3" x 5" index cards
- ❏ 12" x 18" white paper
- ❏ pencils
- ❏ red, blue, and yellow markers

PIET MONDRIAN CREATIONS

A variation on this project can be related to the later works of Piet Mondrian. Even if you are not familiar with this artist by name, a quick glance at any book or website about him will probably look familiar anyway. These pieces would make great visual aids in your classroom. His most famous style involved using bold horizontal and vertical lines in black to create squares and rectangles. He then filled in some of these shapes with primary colors (red, yellow, and blue). You might have the students do a related work. One method I have used is as follows.

Procedure

1. Give each student an index card and a sheet of white paper.

2. Have students trace the card several times onto the paper, overlapping or not, until they create an interesting, balanced design. You might require your students to keep the card only in a horizontal or vertical orientation or allow them to angle it.

3. Then they fill in selected parts with markers in primary colors.

Symmetry

A variety of projects can reinforce the concept of symmetry. One of the easiest involves simply folding a sheet of paper in half. Students open the sheet, place tempera paint in thick splotches, dots, or lines on one half of the paper, close the sheet, and rub, thus transferring the image to the opposite half as a sort of print. They simply repeat the process until they have created an interesting design. I do this project as a color-mixing lesson, so I limit the students to red, yellow, and blue paint, which avoids the muddying that can occur with other color choices.

SYMMETRY AND LINE IN STRING-PULL ART

A corollary project involves kite string and watered-down tempera paint and is a good exercise in line quality. It works well with young children, but students of virtually any age will enjoy it or one of its variations. Wonderful symmetrical patterns result from this procedure, as well as lively calligraphic lines that display a great deal of movement (see figure 29).

Although I have placed this project with others involving symmetry, it is actually part of my first-grade unit on line. At the beginning of the unit, we define *line* as "the path of a moving point." We discuss the fact that artists and mathematicians talk about lines in slightly different ways. In math, lines have one dimension and they are endless. We cannot see things that have only one dimension, and infinite lines are impossible to draw, so even mathematicians use line segments. Like mathematicians, artists may use line to indicate a border or to show movement or direction. Line itself could be a wonderful topic for the integration of math and art.

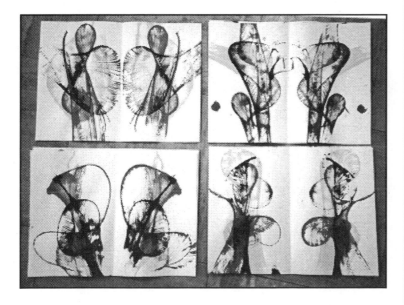

Figure 29. String-pull projects yield fascinating abstract designs and are enjoyable for students of almost any age.

Symmetry and Line In String-Pull Art

Lesson Summary

Students arrange string dipped in primary-colored paint on half of a creased sheet of paper. They fold the paper over and pull the string out under pressure to create a design.

Purpose

To use line expressively; to create abstract, symmetrical designs.

Materials

- ❑ wide, shallow paint containers (3 per work area)
- ❑ red, blue, and yellow tempera paint mixed to a thick, inky consistency (not too watery)
- ❑ 2' lengths of kite string
- ❑ 9" x 12" white construction paper
- ❑ paper towels

Procedure

1. Place containers of red, yellow, and blue tempera paint at each work area, and drape a two-foot length of kite string in each container, making sure that a few inches of one end hangs outside the paint.

2. Have each student select a partner. The students take turns being the artist.

3. The artist takes a piece of white construction paper and folds it in half widthwise into 6″ x 9″ halves. The artist writes his or her name on the outside, then opens the paper and places it with the inside facing up.

4. Starting with the yellow paint, the artist picks the string up by the clean end and holds it over the container. Then pinching the top of the painted end lightly between the thumb and forefinger of the other hand, the pupil pulls up on the string, keeping it over the container. This strips off excess paint. (Students should not pinch too tightly or they will remove too much paint and the project will not work well.)

5. The artist then places the painted part of the string over one half of the paper in an interesting swirl pattern, leaving the clean end hanging off the edge of the paper. The student closes the paper, and the partner presses down firmly on top with both hands, fingers splayed, while the artist pulls the string out. The artist should pull straight out, not up. The pressure should be strong enough to offer some resistance but not so strong as to prevent pulling the string out. (An older student or adult doing this project without a partner can use a large, heavy book to press down on the paper.)

6. The artist returns the yellow string to its paint, opens the paper, and repeats the process with the red paint and then with the blue. (This order will prevent the colors from contaminating each other and muddying the strings.)

7. The students continue taking turns being artist and partner until time runs out. (Provide paper towels so the artist can wipe off his or her hands between colors and before pressing on the partner's paper.)

Variations

You can probably imagine several versions of this project. One interesting twist involves using only black ink or paint and then trying to find a recognizable image in the result. Once the student finds such an image, he or she can enhance it with black marker.

SPLIT-FACE ART

A much more difficult symmetry project involves the additional concept of graphing. This is a relatively common project, although different art teachers use different approaches, depending upon the point they are trying to emphasize.

Instructional tip: This project works with any bilaterally symmetrical object. Some drawing skill is helpful, so non-art teachers may wish to use a less complex subject than a face. You could add science content by using any bilaterally symmetrical plant, organ, or animal.

Procedure

1. Discuss the fact that although human faces are conceptually symmetrical, they are not technically so. I happen to have some terrific photos that prove the point. If you have access to a computer and photo-manipulation program, a great way to demonstrate this is to take a full-face photo, divide it in half, delete the right side, and replace it with a flipped version of the left half. Then repeat the process, deleting the left half and replacing it with a flip of the right half. Neither "new" portrait will look like the original face, and they certainly will not look like each other.

2. After a discussion of facial proportions (see page 82), pass out drawing paper.

3. Have students orient the paper in vertical, or portrait, position. Instruct them to measure halfway across the top of the page and make a dot, then to do the same at the bottom. Be sure they measure from the same side of the page for each dot. They connect the dots with a light pencil line and thus bisect the paper vertically.

4. Using a pencil and ruler, divide the photo of the face in half as accurately as possible. Have students cut out the half you indicate and center it on the line they have drawn on the paper. They glue it in place using a glue stick, being very careful not to get glue on the other side of the page.

Split-Face Art
Lesson Summary
Students paste a half photograph of a face (or any bilaterally symmetrical object) on one side of a sheet of paper. Using careful measurement, they graph out the other half of the face on the blank side of the paper to draw a full face.

Purpose
To reinforce the concept that every point must have two references to be accurately located; to improve drawing ability; to focus on real human features.

Materials
- magazine or newspaper photos that show large, clear, full faces unobstructed by hands, sunglasses, words, and so on (have students bring in)
- computer and photo-manipulation program; e.g., Adobe Photoshop (optional)
- 9" x 12" white drawing paper
- pencils
- rulers
- scissors
- glue sticks (not liquid glue)

5. As I do this project, the next steps are purely mathematical. Because we are trying to achieve perfect symmetry, we begin by virtually graphing the blank side of the page. I explain that, just as students have learned in math, locating a point requires two references, one horizontal and one vertical. For example:

> If students are trying to draw the eye, they will want to find two or three reference points. They must measure from the center line to the inside corner of the eye on the "photo" side, then make a small dot an equal distance away from the center line on the blank side. But this is not enough. They must also measure down from the top of the page to the same spot on each side and adjust their dot accordingly. They repeat the process for the outside of the white of the eye. For some students, these two reference points will be enough. Others may need to locate the top or the bottom of the eye, or both.

6. Working in this way, have students create the lips, the bottom of the nose, the eyebrows, the facial line, and so on. The measurements must be extremely accurate. An error as small as $^1/_{16}''$ can be a big problem when working on this scale.

7. After sketching in the various lines of the face lightly, the student finishes the picture by shading it appropriately (see figure 30).

Instructional tip: If you feel unsure of your ability to help with accurate shading, you could simply choose a subject that is purely linear, such as a diagram from a science or nature book.

Figure 30. Split-face projects combine symmetry with graphing.

POSITIVE AND NEGATIVE SHAPES

Procedure

1. Have students fold a piece of paper carefully in half widthwise to make a little "booklet."

2. Tell them to write their name in a corner on the outside. Have them open the paper and fold the top half back so that it is now underneath and only one-half of the paper shows. (Once again they have a little booklet, but now their name is on the inside.)

3. Have students cover the half of the paper facing up with a solid layer of chalkboard chalk. They should hold the piece up to the light at different angles to be sure it is totally covered. Also caution them to make sure their hand does not brush off the chalk as they work.

Instructional tip: We use white chalk so that nothing detracts from the symmetry of the finished piece, but be aware that this makes it very difficult to see places that have been missed. Any color chalk will do, so you might want to use yellow or some other pale tone. Working on a magazine or other padded surface may facilitate applying the chalk and crayon (next step), but cover the magazine so that the print does not rub off onto the paper.

---

4. Have students cover the layer of chalk completely with a heavy and solid layer of crayon that has a dark value, such as black or blue-violet. Students should try not to remove chalk as they do this. In addition, if they press too hard with the crayon, they will push up little mounds of chalk dust that will cause flaking. (Be sure they crayon the side with the chalk, not the clean half of the page.)

5. When students open the paper up, the back side should have nothing but their name on it, and the front side should be half blank and half colored. Have them fold the blank half over the chalk/crayon half so that the crayoned half is now inside the booklet and the fold is vertical, not across the top or bottom

Positive and Negative Shapes

Lesson Summary
Students coat a half sheet of paper with chalk, then crayon. They fold the paper over and draw on the outside, causing the crayon to lift off and form a symmetrical design.

Purpose
To emphasize positive and negative shapes; to reinforce the concept of symmetry.

Materials
- ❑ white chalkboard chalk
- ❑ black or dark-colored (e.g., blue-violet) crayons
- ❑ sharp pencils
- ❑ 9" x 12" white construction paper or copier paper
- ❑ magazines or newspapers for padding (optional)

Mirror-Image Symmetry

Lesson Summary

Students draw half an object on one color of paper. They cut out the half object and paste the paper from which the shape was cut on one half of a large sheet of paper that has a contrasting color. Then they flip and paste the half-image on the other half of the background, creating a bilateral object, with one half positive and the other half negative.

Purpose

To explore symmetry; to explore positive and negative space.

Materials

- ❏ 2 highly contrasting colors of construction paper, one color 3″ x 6″ and the other 6″ x 6″ (or 6″ x 9″ and 9″ x 12″, respectively)
- ❏ pencils
- ❏ scissors
- ❏ glue sticks or paste

6. With a sharp pencil, students draw a design on the outside of the folded page, being sure to draw solid, filled-in shapes or thick lines. The crayon should not only transfer to the white half of the paper, but "lift" completely off the dark side (if it is completely chalked), creating a symmetrical result that emphasizes positive and negative shapes.

Instructional tip: Warn students that they cannot "shade" or erase the pencil marks—shapes are either black or white. Also warn them that the pencil must not be sharp enough, nor the pressure hard enough, to puncture the paper.

MIRROR-IMAGE SYMMETRY

The final two symmetry projects can be adapted in a variety of ways. In its simplest form, you can make it very small.

Materials tip: If you do this project in a different size, be sure that the smaller piece of paper occupies half the area of the larger piece.

Procedure

1. Have students place the smaller piece of paper in portrait—that is, vertical—orientation.

2. Starting from one long edge, they draw the outline of half an object, such as half a house, half a heart, or half a butterfly (see figure 31). (Make sure they choose a simple outline that they can cut out accurately.) Instruct them to fill the page nicely, with fairly even amounts of *positive* space (the shape they draw) and *negative* space (the background, or shape left over). The outline should end on the same side it started from.

Figure 31. This simple piece was created by cutting half a butterfly out of black paper. The black "background" was pasted on one half of a white piece of paper, then the cutout of the half butterfly was flipped and pasted on the other half of the white paper, aligned to create a symmetrical image.

3. Students cut out the shape carefully in a continuous cut, keeping the background (negative space) completely intact.

4. They place the larger piece of paper in landscape (horizontal) orientation.

5. Students align the uncut long edge of the *negative* shape carefully against one of the short sides of the large sheet of paper and glue it down.

6. Students then place the cutout shape back into position, like a puzzle piece. After spreading glue on the side facing up, they flip the cutout, like turning the page of a book, onto the other half of the large piece of paper. The two images should meet at the center line, with the two halves aligning exactly.

MIRROR-IMAGE SCENES

You may wish to do a more involved version of this project for older students.

Materials tip: If you do this project in a different size, be sure that the smaller piece of paper occupies half the area of the larger piece.

Procedure

1. On a 9" x 12" piece of paper in portrait orientation, the students draw a picture or design lightly in pencil, using only shapes (that is, closed figures). No shape may touch any other shape or an outside edge, although there may be shapes that are entirely inside other shapes.

Instructional tip: Remind students that they will have to cut out these shapes accurately, so they should not be too small or convoluted.

---

2. Again, the background needs to remain one continuous piece, which means that one cannot cut in from the edge to cut out interior shapes. To make cutting easier for elementary students, I "start" the

Mirror-Image Scenes
Lesson Summary
Students draw a picture or design using only shapes. They carefully cut out the shapes without damaging the background. They arrange the cutouts on one half of a large piece of paper in a contrasting color, then paste the background on the other half to create a bilaterally symmetrical work.

Purpose
To explore symmetry; to explore positive and negative spaces.

Materials
- ❑ 2 highly contrasting colors of construction paper, one color 3" x 6" and the other 6" x 6" (or 6" x 9" and 9" x 12", respectively)
- ❑ pencils
- ❑ scissors
- ❑ paper clips
- ❑ utility knife
- ❑ glue sticks or paste

shapes by making a small slit with a sharp blade along each outline. This avoids big puncture holes and a lot of tearing.

3. The students cut out the shapes carefully, being sure not to trim any paper off the shapes or to cut through the negative space in any way. When they are finished, they should have one continuous negative (background) shape and all of the cutout pieces, which when placed back together like a puzzle, should reveal no gaps.

4. The students take a piece of 12″ x 18″ paper in a contrasting color, and place it in landscape (horizontal) position. They take the negative (background) piece from step 3 and place it carefully on one half of the large sheet, so that it lines up along either the left or right edge. (Students may wish to use paper clips to prevent the background from moving while they work.)

5. This project has multiple individual pieces that must be placed in exactly the right location to create a symmetrical drawing. To place all these pieces correctly by measurement would require extremely precise measuring in two directions, and even a small measurement error would ruin the symmetrical effect. Therefore, a much simpler procedure, and one less prone to error, is to use the background piece as a stencil within which to place the cutout pieces for gluing. This will ensure that all the cutouts are correctly placed. First, you will need to identify whether any students have cut shapes-within-shapes, such as the window shape cut within the house shape in figure 32. As you can see, these need to alternate: light background, dark house, light window, and vice versa. This is accomplished in step 6. If no one has shapes-within-shapes, you can skip to step 7.

Figure 32. Second-grader Neil Shah created this delightful piece using essentially the same technique as for the butterfly in the previous figure.

6. **To place a shape within another shape:** Have students separate out all the pieces that belong to shapes-within-shapes. First they will want to put the outside piece (e.g., the house shape) in place in the background. Now they have a space exactly where the inside piece (e.g., the window) fits. They spread glue in the hole and fit the window piece into place, then repeat this process for any other shapes-within-shapes. When all these interior pieces have been glued, they flip the background over the center line, as if turning the page of a book, and line it up on the other edge of the large paper. (Thus, it is now in mirror-image orientation: back-to-front as well as on the other half of the sheet.)

7. Students place all the remaining cutout pieces into the spaces from which they were cut. Now they simply pick up each cutout, spread glue in the opening, and fit the piece back into place. (If a piece has a hole in it, the student must put the glue on the back of the piece, rather than in the opening, so that the glue won't show through.)

8. When all the interior shapes have been glued down, students cover the background carefully with glue. They then flip the background over the center line, as if turning the page of a book, and glue it carefully in place. (For those students who had shapes-within-shapes, they are now back on the side where they started.)

Perspective

Even if you have no background in perspective drawing, there are some brief exercises that you can do that will help your students (and you) discover some of its components. I use the following projects and exercises as the culminating activities for my unit on the Renaissance (see page 88 for background information). Work in perspective is essentially a study of geometry. For example, perspective lines may meet at one, two, or three points. The fact that the relative size of shapes or objects varies as a function of the viewer's distance from them is used to create the illusion of depth in paintings.

 Suggested Resource

Marc Frantz was trained as an artist and currently teaches upper-level mathematics at Indiana University/Purdue University at Indianapolis. In his workshops and classes, he uses art to illuminate math and vice versa, and he includes some wonderful perspective exercises in his curriculum. Frantz's website has great perspective exercises, as well as activities with fractals: http://www.math.iupui.edu/mtc/Art/Art.html.

DEMONSTRATION: MOVING OBJECTS FARTHER AWAY

The easiest exercises—and ones you can do with even the youngest students—involve the concept that as things move away from us, they *appear* to get smaller.

Version 1

1. Have the students hold their hands in front of their face with the palms about four or five inches from their eyes.

2. Have them close the left eye and, keeping the left hand in front of it, move the right hand straight out in front as far as it will go.

3. The right hand will now appear to be much smaller than the left. Have them bring the hand slowly back in until both hands appear the same size again.

Version 2

Another example of this phenomenon requires a very large room, such as a gym or a long hallway. It could also be done outdoors. We do this near one end of a very long hallway at the opposite end of which is a door. I stand in front of my students with my back to the door many yards in front of it. I ask them if I appear small enough to fit through the door. I then walk slowly backwards until the students tell me I have "shrunk" enough. Outdoors, you could become much bigger than a tree or smaller than a shrub or mailbox. Most older students have probably "pinched" a distant friend between their thumb and forefinger. (Having students take photographs demonstrating such optical illusions can be an appealing project.)

HORIZON LINES AND VANISHING POINTS

If you have a large interior room or long hall with a suspended ceiling or other type of grid pattern like a tiled floor, try this exercise and the Drawing in Perspective Lines activity.

1. Have the students stand up straight in the middle of the room or a hallway and visually mark a point directly in front of them at their eye level. (In perspective, this eye level is termed the *horizon line*.)

2. They should note how counters, door tops, baseboards, locker tops, and the edges of other forms that range along the sides of the space appear to slant up or down and inward toward that point. The spot at which all the lines appear to converge is the *vanishing point*.

3. Have students slowly lower themselves to the ground. What happens to all the lines parallel to the ground?

4. Have them move slowly sideways to the right or left, still facing straight ahead. In both cases, the vanishing point should appear to move with them.

DRAWING IN PERSPECTIVE LINES

To help them visualize this effect, or to reinforce the concept, try the following.

Procedure

1. Stand in the center of a hallway or long room and, using a digital camera, take a photograph down its length (see figure 33). Be sure that the vertical lines in your photo are truly vertical. (To illustrate two-point perspective, photograph the corner of a large box or building.)

2. Enlarge your photo on the computer to fill an 8 ½" x 11" piece of paper and make a copy for each student.

3. Using a yardstick and a pencil, students simply draw right on the copy, extending ceiling (or roof) lines, floor lines, tops of doors or windows, lines of brick or siding, and so on, to observe how lines that are in fact parallel to each other and to the ground merge at a single point in one's view of them (see figure 33).

Drawing In Perspective Lines

Lesson Summary
On a photocopy of an actual structure, students draw in vertical lines to observe how they meet at the vanishing point.

Purpose
To visually demonstrate perspective.

Materials
- ❏ digital camera
- ❏ photo software
- ❏ copy machine
- ❏ yardsticks and pencils

Figure 33. This photo of our hallway has lines drawn in showing how they meet at the vanishing point. This is an example of one-point perspective.

Scenery in Perspective

Lesson Summary

Students trace lines of a view on clear plastic, concentrating on straight perspective lines. They observe how changes in their position affect the convergence lines.

Purpose

To visually demonstrate that lines and shapes are affected by one's position.

Materials

☐ a window or large piece of clear plastic (e.g., Plexiglas)

☐ dry-erase marker

☐ a view with perspective

SCENERY IN PERSPECTIVE

Procedure

1. If you have a view out your classroom window that offers an interesting perspective, you could do this exercise right on the window. Otherwise, you will need to have students hold a large piece of Plexiglas in front of an interesting interior view. Have them rest the Plexiglas on a desk or table and precisely mark its location so it does not move. Also remind the students who are holding the Plexiglas to stand very still.

2. Using a dry-erase marker, a student traces the view onto the glass or plastic, following the edges of the walls, doors, and other objects as accurately as possible. This is much harder than it looks, because the slightest change in the artist's position changes the horizon line or vanishing point(s) or both.

3. You might draw the lines yourself and then have the students find the exact position they must assume for the lines to match the view, or you could have each one try drawing the perspective lines themselves or in groups.

STILL LIFE

As a final project, my students create a still life using objects that reflect the simple forms of spheres, cones, cubes, and cylinders. You can do a simplified version of a still life without art training.

Procedure

1. Create a still life using objects with simple forms. Place the objects on a table so that they overlap slightly (see figure 34 on page 150). Try to have a single, strong light source coming from the side. Photograph the grouping with a digital camera set on black-and-white mode. Choose a position that

allows you to see the top of the tallest object but is not high enough above the grouping to throw you into three-point (looking from above) perspective. (If you do not have a digital camera, you could scan a regular photograph and print it in grayscale.)

2. Enlarge the photo to fill an 8 ½″ x 11″ page, make a print, and photocopy enough for all the students. Make sure you can see each item clearly in the copies.

3. Have the students rub the back of their photocopy with a soft pencil until it is covered with graphite. Then have them center that paper, picture side up, on a piece of 9″ x 12″ drawing paper. (If drawing paper is not available, use 8 ½″ x 11″ copier paper.) They should secure the two pieces in some way that will not harm the drawing paper, such as paper clipping them together or taping lightly with tiny bits of masking tape. They then clip this arrangement in turn to a long piece of newspaper or center it along the bottom of two pieces of 12″ x 18″ manila taped together to produce a 12″ x 36″ piece. (The horizon lines and vanishing point[s] will extend onto the newspaper or manila paper, allowing students to replace their drawing in position if it slips.) It is a good idea to have them trace around the drawing paper lightly on the manila and to mark the corners of the photo with dots on the drawing paper, in case the paper or photo slip as they are working.

4. Using a yardstick and a sharp pencil, they should carefully trace all the contours of the objects, pressing firmly to transfer their tracing to the sheet below. Have them extend appropriate lines until they find the vanishing point or points. To find the horizon line, they should either connect the two vanishing points they will find in a setup like figure 34 or draw a line parallel to the top and bottom of the page that passes through a single vanishing point. Students may lift the top sheet occasionally to make sure the lines are transferring lightly onto the drawing paper, but they must not move it out of position. Even though the bottom of a cylinder like the mug in figure 34 does not show as an oval, they should draw the entire implied oval anyway to illustrate circular perspective.

Still Life

Lesson Summary

Working with a photocopy of a simple still life, students cover the back with pencil, then trace around the shapes to transfer their outlines to a second piece of paper. They identify the vanishing point or points and the horizon line. Then using the original photocopy as a model, they shade the drawing to create a three-dimensional effect.

Purpose

To apply perspective in a simple still-life drawing.

Materials

- ❏ digital camera or a regular photo and a scanner
- ❏ objects with simple cylindrical, conical, or cubic forms (e.g., coffee mug, Rubik's cube, tennis ball)
- ❏ flood lamp or other light source
- ❏ photocopy machine
- ❏ soft pencils
- ❏ 9″ x 12″ drawing paper
- ❏ paper clips or masking tape
- ❏ newspaper, or 2 sheets of 12″ x 18″ manila paper taped together, per student
- ❏ yardsticks
- ❏ sharp pencils

5. When all the lines look correct, students remove the top sheet and erase any unnecessary lines from the drawing paper. Then, using the photo as a guide, they shade their drawing. Students should not darken the light transferred lines, but only make the shading agree with the photo. (If you look at a real ball or mug, it does not have dark outlines.)

6. Have students leave the drawing paper attached to the manila or newspaper until the project is complete. They may need to restore lines that get smudged or erased, and the guidelines and vanishing point(s) on the big paper will help.

7. There should be some sort of table line behind the objects; if there is not one in the original photo, then students should add it.

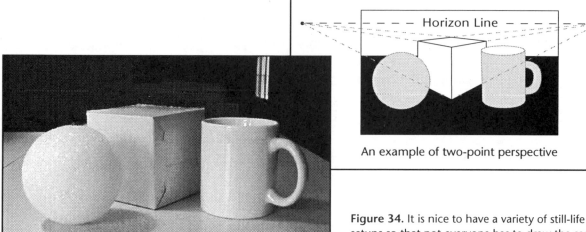

Figure 34. It is nice to have a variety of still-life setups so that not everyone has to draw the same thing, but keep them simple, as in this example. The cube is in two-point perspective.

Tessellation

A tessellation is a design in which there is no leftover space—all the positive shapes fit together like a puzzle. A checkerboard is one example, and the geometric patterns used in much Arabic art and architecture provide many others.

Suggested Resources

- You are probably familiar with the works of M. C. Escher. An artist and a mathematician, he is famous for his creative use of tessellated designs and the optical illusions he devised through his complete mastery of the theories of perspective. Posters and slides of his work are easily obtainable.

- For lesson ideas, check *Mosaic and Tessellated Patterns: How to Create Them* by John Willson, or any similar source.

INDEX CARD TESSELLATION

Even young children can do a simple tessellation. Here is an extremely basic project that Jan Kendall and Elaine Sandy have Sycamore first graders do.

Procedure

1. On an index card have students draw a shape that begins and ends at the top of the card and has the flat edge of the card as its top.

2. Have the students cut out the shape and slide it down below the bottom edge of the card, positioning the flat edge at the top of the shape carefully against the bottom edge of the index card, directly below the cutout, and tape it in place. The card now somewhat resembles a puzzle piece, with a shape cut out of the top and the identical shape extending from the bottom (see figure 35a).

3. Students place the card in the upper corner of a piece of construction paper, lining up the top and one side of the card with the edges of the paper. They trace the parts of the shape not formed by the edges of the paper.

4. They then move the card down the side of the page until the cutout at the top of the card lines up on the previous tracing of the bottom part of the shape. They trace the parts that are not already formed by the previous tracing and the edge of the paper.

5. They continue in this manner until they reach the bottom of the construction paper. If there is not room at the bottom to draw the entire shape, they draw only as much of it as will fit.

6. They move the card back to the top of the construction paper and place it exactly against the drawn side of the first shape. They trace around the shape and repeat the process until the entire page is filled (see figure 35b).

7. Ask students whether their shapes look like anything—perhaps a bird or a train. They might choose to embellish their drawings à la Escher by adding a

Index Card Tessellation

Lesson Summary

Students create a "puzzle piece" shape from an index card and use this as a stencil, tracing around it repeatedly to fill a page with a repetitive design.

Purpose

To introduce the concept of tessellation; to reinforce the concept of positive space.

Materials

- ☐ 3" x 5" index cards
- ☐ pencils
- ☐ scissors
- ☐ 12" x 18" construction paper
- ☐ tape
- ☐ crayons, markers, or colored pencils

few details to reinforce the resemblance (such as giving the "bird" an eye). Students now may color in the shapes, using an alternating pattern of contrasting colors (see figure 35c).

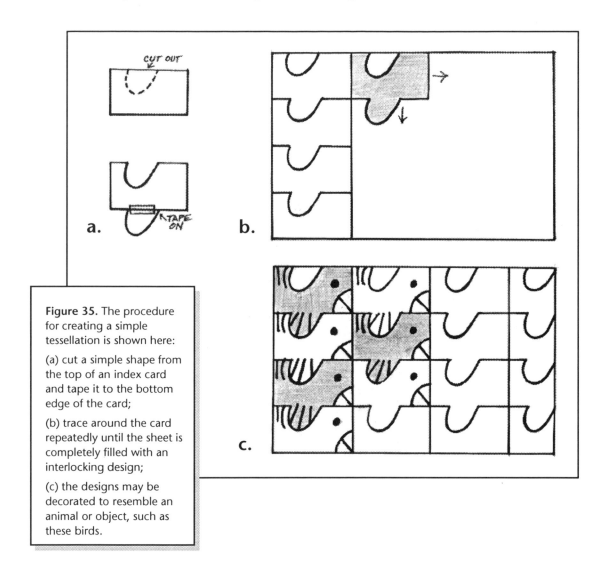

Figure 35. The procedure for creating a simple tessellation is shown here:

(a) cut a simple shape from the top of an index card and tape it to the bottom edge of the card;

(b) trace around the card repeatedly until the sheet is completely filled with an interlocking design;

(c) the designs may be decorated to resemble an animal or object, such as these birds.

Variation

Once students have the basic idea, they could cut pieces from more than one edge of the card. Or you might choose to focus on one of the specific types of tessellation.

Ratios and Focusing

One mathematical operation with frequent application in art is the figuring of ratios. On page 56, I describe an activity in which we figure dimensions from a floor plan. One of the projects I offer as a culminating activity for our unit on Formalism requires students to use such an equation, so if you are looking for practical applications of mathematical concepts, perhaps you could use or adapt it.

ENLARGEMENT USING RATIOS

An obvious application of ratios is for changing the scale of a drawing. This activity and the next offer two methods for enlargement.

Procedure

1. Students cut two L-shaped corners from a piece of heavy paper. Both legs of each L should be 2″–3″ long and about ½″–¾″ wide. It is very important that the interior lines of each L be straight and that they form a true right angle.

2. Have students bring in a photograph or illustration from a book or magazine. They overlap the two L's to form a frame on top of the illustration. Demonstrate how the interior size and shape of the frame may be adjusted depending upon how they move and overlap the legs of the L's. Photographers sometimes use this method when cropping photos.

3. Students move the little frame over the surface of the object or picture, adjusting the size and orientation until they find an interesting composition. Ideally, this small section should enclose an interesting arrangement of shapes that makes an abstract design, giving no clue as to the nature of the actual subject.

4. Once they have selected a view they like, students tape the two L's together to fix the frame at that size, then affix the frame to the picture in a way that will keep it from moving but will not damage the subject.

Enlargement Using Ratios

Lesson Summary
Students select a small-sized design, then use ratio calculations to enlarge it to fit a full-sized sheet of paper

Purpose
To use the concept of ratio to change the scale of an art project; to reinforce the concept of ratios.

Materials
- ❑ tagboard or heavy paper
- ❑ photograph or illustration (student-provided)
- ❑ scissors
- ❑ pencil
- ❑ ruler
- ❑ masking tape
- ❑ 12″ x 18″ drawing paper
- ❑ tempera, watercolors, crayons, or markers to color drawing

5. Have students measure the interior dimensions of the frame and, if need be, adjust the size of the frame to dimensions that are straightforward for calculation, such as 1″ x ½″ or ½″ x ¾″.

6. Students now enlarge the design onto a piece of drawing paper. For illustrative purposes in the following discussion, I will assume students are enlarging a ½″ x ¾″ design to fit a 12″ x 18″ sheet of paper. Before they begin drawing, students must ensure that the drawing paper is in the same proportions as the small frame, cutting the large sheet to the correct proportions if necessary. Here is the equation:

width of interior frame
is to *length of interior frame*
as *width of paper* **is to** *x*

For example: ½″ is to ¾″ as 12″ is to *x*

$$\frac{\frac{1}{2}}{\frac{3}{4}} = \frac{12}{x}$$

In this case, *x* equals 18, so you would not have to cut anything. If the value of *x* exceeds 18, reverse the procedure and make *x* the width.

7. Once the paper is cut to size, students start measuring various relationships within the design. Imagine that one of the shapes extends ⅛″ from the left-hand side of the base of the frame, and that the bottom and top are the ¾″ sides. In order to see how far the shape must extend in the enlarged drawing, they would calculate:

length of shape **is to** *length of frame*
as x is to *length of full-size drawing*

$$\frac{\frac{1}{8}}{\frac{3}{4}} = \frac{x}{18} \qquad x = 3$$

Students continue in this manner until they have plotted out all the major relationships and sketched a full-size picture that matches the one inside the frame.

8. They may then color the drawing with any appropriate material—tempera, watercolors, crayons, colored pencils, or markers. It is not necessary to be true to the original colors: bright, bold colors and subtle variations can both be interesting, and strong, solid coverage works better than a light application of the medium.

GRID ENLARGEMENTS

A grid enlargement is an enjoyable way to reinforce several math concepts. I have used grid enlargement as the culminating activity for a unit on twentieth-century Realism, but you could focus on how any number of artists have used this device through the ages. For example, the early Egyptians had strict rules for the proportions of their figures. When placed on a grid, the entire figure was $18\frac{1}{2}$ squares tall. From the bottom of the foot to the knee was 6 squares, the knee to the shoulder was 10, the neck and face were 2, and the wig was $\frac{1}{2}$ square. Whenever they wanted to change the scale of the figure, they simply drew the squares larger or smaller and filled them in accordingly. Artists have frequently used this system to transfer their smaller sketches onto larger canvases. At the Art Institute of Chicago, you can see a somewhat unfinished painting by Giorgio Vasari entitled *The Temptation of Saint Jerome* where the underlying grid is still visible. The great Renaissance artist Albrecht Dürer, among others, used a frame with an adjustable grid of strings to aid him in drawing perspective.

If you want your students to use this approach themselves, try this lesson.

Procedure

1. Select a small subject as basic or as complex as you wish. (In math classes at Sycamore, the students chose simple one-panel cartoons from the newspaper, and in my class we used photographs.)

2. Students now need a grid over the subject. You could have them draw the grid with a ruler and pen or pencil, but I have found that this task takes time and that students have difficulty measuring and drawing parallel lines accurately. As a time-saver, I photocopy graph paper onto clear overhead projector film. I then cut the film into pieces that fit the size of students' subjects. They simply tape these over their photo or cartoon.

Grid Enlargements

Lesson Summary

Students enlarge a simple photo or drawing. They draw a grid on the subject, then draw a larger, proportional grid on drawing paper. By duplicating what is in each square of the grid on the subject, they create an enlarged drawing.

Purpose

To use the concept of grid enlargement to change the scale of an artwork; to reinforce the concept of a grid.

Materials

- ❑ drawing to enlarge (e.g., a simple photograph or cartoon drawing)
- ❑ rulers
- ❑ pencils
- ❑ ¼" graph paper
- ❑ clear overhead projector film
- ❑ photocopier
- ❑ drawing paper up to 12" x 18"

Instructional tip: If you want to reinforce the actual measuring and drawing of the lines but do not want to damage the drawings or photographs students are working from, you could have your students draw their own grids on acetate with permanent markers.

---

3. Now students prepare to transfer the subject to a larger piece of drawing paper. To begin, they count the number of horizontal and vertical squares on their subject. (For example, a 4″ x 6″ photograph divided into a ¼″ grid yields 16 squares in one direction and 24 in the other.) The student must grid the drawing paper accordingly, which requires more math. Assume the paper is 12″ x 18″:

$$\frac{12}{16} = \text{}^3/_4 \quad \text{and} \quad \frac{18}{24} = \text{}^3/_4$$

Thus, marking the page off with lines ³/₄″ apart will yield the perfect number of squares. (Obviously, not all solutions will be this tidy.)

Instructional tip: Once again, I saved my students time and frustration by providing paper with the grid photocopied onto the back. I created several different scales, and they had to do the math to calculate which grid would work best. The paper is thin enough that if the student works on a light-colored surface, the lines will show through on the front. I mounted the finished project on black cardboard, so the grid lines are not visible.

---

4. The students simply duplicate what they see in each square of the small original as accurately as possible in the corresponding larger squares of the drawing paper. This involves a lot of counting and concentration. You might suggest that they transfer the outlines of the main shapes first, so that mistakes can be caught quickly.

5. When the drawing is complete, they simply color or shade the result appropriately.

MORE FUN WITH RATIOS

Commercial grid puzzles: You have probably seen a variation of this lesson in puzzle books. A blank grid is provided with one axis of squares labeled A, B, C, D, and so on, and the other labeled 1, 2, 3, 4, and so forth. Elsewhere on the page is a corresponding number of squares with bits of lines and shapes in them in no particular order but labeled 2B or 9G or whatever. By carefully copying the contents of each square into its counterpart in the blank grid, you create a picture.

Image distortions: You can create interesting distortions by using a grid with lines at various distances apart or lines that are not parallel to each other or to the edges of the page. The lines on the original will form squares, but on the drawing paper, they might be diamonds or parallelograms or completely random shapes.

Anamorphic drawings: Anamorphic pictures are distorted images that appear in realistic proportion only when viewed from a particular angle or in a cylindrical mirror placed in the center of the drawing. You can create anamorphic pictures by distorting the drawing grid in particular ways. Hans Holbein the Younger includes a wonderful example of this technique in his painting *The Ambassadors*. When viewed from the proper angle, the odd shape in the center of the floor becomes a skull. For instructions on creating anamorphic art, consult a source such as *The Magic Cylinder Book* by Ivan Moscovich.

Other Possible Projects

Quilt squares: Creating quilt squares, in either fabric or paper, can be a wonderful way to explore geometric concepts. Any book on quilt making will offer a wealth of patterns to illustrate geometric principles.

String art: String art is another approach. A wide variety of curves can be created from short segments of straight lines. By plotting out these lines and sewing them onto cardboard, you can devise a project that emphasizes such art concepts as line, color, value, and contrast as well as mathematical principles. A wonderful source for such lessons is *Curve Stitching: The Art of Sewing Beautiful Mathematical Patterns* by Jon Millington. Susan Vieth and Mary Pleiss have used quilts and string art very successfully in their fourth-grade classrooms at Sycamore.

Fractals: Earlier in the chapter I referred to Marc Frantz. One of the areas he explores on his website is fractals, a form of non-Euclidean geometry described by Benoit Mandelbrot and familiar to many computer programmers and users. Students could use existing fractal programs to design artworks on the computer, or they could create their own. For further information, visit Marc's website at http://www.math.iupui.edu/mtc/Art/Art.html. For another interesting use of fractals in art, you might have your students research the work of Jhane Barnes, a highly successful fashion and furniture designer who uses fractals in the creation of her fabrics. §

CHAPTER 13
Performing Arts

"I try to apply colors like words that shape poems, like notes that shape music."

—Joan Miró

Like literature, the performing arts offer enormous possibilities for projects related to the visual arts. From common terminology—tone color, texture, rhythm, line, movement, contrast, balance—to similar questions of aesthetics and criticism, these subjects offer fertile ground for integration. Showing the similarities among these subjects can be extremely effective in engaging students who play an instrument, sing, act, or dance.

Music

DRAWING TO MUSIC

Each year, the Junior Group of the Women's Committee of the Indianapolis Symphony Orchestra sponsors a Symphony in Color contest, in which young people illustrate five pieces played by the symphony during the previous season. You might check with organizations in your state to see if they have a similar project. Whether your students enter such a competition or not, the concept is easily adaptable to any age group.

Much of the assignment is conducive to an independent project. At Sycamore, the music teacher presents the selections to the eligible students in her class and the artwork is done as an elective after-school activity through the art department. After the students hear the music, they sketch their visual interpretations and bring them to me. We talk about such topics as composition, imagery, and what medium the student would like to use. There are three general approaches to this assignment (see figure 36):

Figure 36. Jessica Berger used touches of gold to highlight this dramatic piece reflecting a Russian musical composition.

> "Art classes teach you more than just how to draw and how to color. They teach you how to appreciate art, all of the arts. I don't think my interest in music would be as great without art classes."
>
> —Josh, Sycamore student

- To interpret the mood or rhythm of the piece abstractly, using color or line or texture to express the music symbolically
- To reflect the story line of the selection (if it has one) using appropriate imagery
- To focus on depicting the musical instruments heard in the selection

The easiest way to adapt this approach is simply to play a musical selection in class and have the students draw or paint or sculpt to it. You might play the piece without providing any information and then see if any of the interpretations reflect the actual intent of the composer. (It is helpful to have a brief biography of the composer and a critical interpretation of the work on hand. You could provide this information or assign the students to research the answers to specific questions.)

Suggested Resources

For younger children, it is nice to have at least a few choices that have a story or evoke strong visual images, such as these:

- *The Dance of the Little Swans* by Tchaikovsky
- *The Carnival of the Animals,* especially the segment entitled "The Aquarium," by Saint-Saëns
- "Mars" from *The Planets* by Holst
- any selection from *Pictures at an Exhibition* by Mussorgsky
- "Dawn" from the *Peer Gynt Suite* by Grieg
- any piece from *The Wand of Youth* by Elgar
- *La Mer* by Debussy
- "Sabre Dance" from *Gayane* by Khachaturian
- Of course, you are not limited to classical music. You could use anything from Yanni to the Beatles, depending upon the nature of the students and the desired outcome. Music from other cultures might be a natural way to engage the interest of certain pupils.

Variations

Matching existing music and art: One possibility would be to have students find an existing work of art that they feel expresses the musical selection and to explain why they chose it (as an oral presentation or essay, for example). Conversely, you could select a work of visual art and have students compose or select musical pieces to accompany it. History teachers could adapt this approach to a specific era; literature teachers might do the same and tie both choices to a particular book or story.

Improvisation to artworks: I am fortunate to have a son who graduated from the Oberlin Conservatory of Music. Each year I have students create an artwork on blank music manuscript sheets. (The works need not have anything to do with music—they can be representational or totally abstract.) My son then improvises music based upon the students' visual work, explaining how the artwork evokes the melodies he is improvising. For example, he might relate a circle on the page to a circle of fifths or use colors to inspire a mood piece. He usually starts by pointing out that one of the primary differences between music and art is that, whereas we can perceive a work of visual art almost instantaneously, music takes place over time. He also explains the difference between *composition* and *improvisation,* a point that has significant applications to the art student. During the course of his presentation, he talks about *line, rhythm, tone color,* and *texture,* as well as the vertical and horizontal aspects of reading music. Perhaps you know or can locate a musician who can give a similar guest lecture.

MUSIC VIDEOS

Paula Fair, the former music teacher at Sycamore, incorporated art into her music classes in a variety of ways. An outstanding educator, she is a firm supporter of solid instruction in visual arts, and she never misses an opportunity to correlate art with music. Paula used this lesson in both second and seventh grades, with the older students completing a more complex animation project.

Procedure

1. Have the class select a favorite folk song or popular song. (You may wish to specify choices related to your curriculum.)

Music Videos

Lesson Summary

Students create a simple video to accompany a folk or popular song.

Purpose

To help students interpret music more deeply; to engage students on several levels; to show relationships between art and music.

Materials

❑ folk song or popular song

❑ video camera with VHS-C film

❑ poster board and markers

2. Divide the song into individual stanzas and assign each stanza to a group of students.

3. Each group illustrates their stanza using large white poster board and colored markers.

4. After all the posters are completed, have students set up the video camera (with teacher supervision).

5. Students measure the camera range on the wall, then hang the illustrations, one at a time, in order.

6. Students focus on the boards one at a time and film each for ten seconds (the camera does not pan), using fade between each board.

7. After the entire series has been filmed, students perform their song to the video. (If a soundtrack is desired, the class could tape their performance and lay the soundtrack on top of the video.)

Instructional tip: This project could be achieved as a collaboration between an art and a music class. It could also be framed as a research or art history project, using actual art from an era concurrent with the folk song.

Variation for Older Students

Students should begin by viewing examples of the three types of stop-motion animation (line, collage, or claymation) and a demonstration of the camera work involved. Divide students into small groups; within each group the students decide how to divide up the responsibilities of camera operation, lighting, and animation. All students can work on the rough drafts or preliminary sketches, then the animator produces the finished drawings. In the experience of Paula's students, most animation styles worked best using three frames per second, or three-second intervals on video. After each project is completely filmed, the students fit their soundtracks to the edited video. Paula usually used original piano or xylophone compositions to make this easier. It would probably be great fun for art and music classes to team up on such a project, with the artists creating the animation then the musicians creating a soundtrack.

NATIVE AMERICAN INSTRUMENTS

This project goes far beyond merely integrating art and music. It would be a great idea for a social studies or language arts culminating activity, and it could be adapted in a wide variety of ways. In Paula's class, fifth-grade students studied various Native American nations and their music, mythology, and instruments. Each student then built a percussion, wind, or string instrument from "found" materials. The project was done in class using materials students obtained off-campus. After the instruments were constructed and tested for playability—a requirement of the assignment—they were decorated using authentic symbols, colors, and materials. Finally, each student created a myth that named and explained the origins of the new instrument. The instrument was then demonstrated while the myth was told during class.

MUSIC MANUSCRIPT ILLUMINATION

Paula did this project in fifth grade, but it is appropriate for older students because it requires that they have significant vocabulary and conceptual understanding. The instructor also needs background in both art and music, so it may be best done as a collaborative venture between the art and music teachers. It also would make a great culminating activity in social studies.

1. After a study of the music of the Middle Ages, introduce students to the concept of prose rhythm—musical rhythm that is dictated by the rhythm of the words. Various poems could be chanted in class, then sung in call-response form to demonstrate this rhythm concept.

2. Discuss the development of early music notation, and show examples of the minima, semibrevis, brevis, longa, and maxima. Dorian, Lydian, mixolydian, Aeolian, and Phrygian modes could be reviewed and demonstrated. Review the three types of chant melodies: syllabic, neumatic, and melismatic chant. Also display examples of illuminations from the Middle Ages.

3. Each student selects a nursery rhyme from a list you provide. Using this rhyme for the prose rhythm, the student develops a plainsong chant based completely on one of the aforementioned modes. The students use a piano or Orff xylophone to help them sketch the melody on staff paper.

4. After the melody has been roughed in, students assign the various neumes to each syllable. In certain appropriate places in the melody, students assign some melismatic or neumatic treatments.

5. After the rough drafts have been completed and approved, students are given parchment-like paper on which a staff and an open space in the upper left-hand corner for the illuminated first letter of the chant have been duplicated.

6. The students complete all neumes with black ink, then produce an illumination in colored marker. All objects in the illumination should be outlined in black ink. (Of course, this should be laid out in pencil first.)

MUSIC AND ART VOCABULARY

As music and art teachers know, their two disciplines share a great deal of vocabulary. Paula always used art elements to introduce musical elements to young students, because using visual symbols often helped these young students imagine musical concepts that exist in time and not space. She explained in simple terms that the music on the page is only a symbol of the music that actually exists over time. She related each musical term to a corresponding art word. Music and art teachers could easily work together to create a single unit on vocabulary. Here are some ideas:

Melody can be visualized as line, moving up, down, or staying the same.

Harmony is symbolized as the primary colors mixing to form secondaries and other colors.

Texture, of course, exists in both disciplines, and the weaving of fabric textures makes a nice analogy to music.

Form and **tone color** also have their counterparts in visual art.

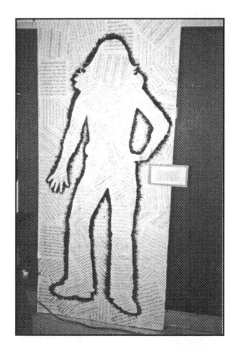

Figure 37. Heather Fraiz created a life-sized reverse silhouette of herself on a collage of music manuscripts as her self-portrait for Eighth-Grade Extravaganza. She adapted a project we had done in second grade.

ILLUSTRATIONS OF MUSICAL INSTRUMENTS OR PERFORMANCES

You could certainly display artworks containing musical references as a quick way to bring visual art into the classroom, to explore music history, and to improve students' recognition of instruments. Incidentally, because music is fleeting, pages of sheet music and instruments were often used as metaphors for life in *vanitas* paintings (see page 112 for an explanation). An interesting artistic use for sheet music is shown in the self-portrait in figure 37.

 Suggested Resources

- Take 5 Art Prints offers an interdisciplinary series called *Art and Music.*
- Egyptian wall paintings and Japanese woodcuts of the Edo period frequently show images of people playing instruments. So does Classical Greek pottery.
- Some paintings you might explore are Jan Vermeer's *The Concert,* Pablo Picasso's *Three Musicians,* Thomas Eakins's *The Concert Singer,* and William Harnett's *Music and Good Luck.*

Dance

Whether or not your school offers dance as a curricular choice, most older students have experienced some form of this art. Some may take tap or ballet lessons, or they may simply dance to popular music. Physical education teachers are increasingly incorporating movement to music into their programs for young children, and football players, for example, are some-times encouraged to take certain dance classes to improve their balance.

SKETCHING A DANCER

In a school where dance is not offered, student dancers may have little opportunity to share their talents. (In fact, depending upon the circumstances, they may even hide their skills.) Several years ago, I had an eighth grader, Courtney, who studied ballet, jazz, modern, and tap dance. Dance was central to her life and she was extremely accomplished. She was kind and confident enough to help me structure the following lesson. If you have such a student, and he or she is willing, you might consider adapting it as a great way to showcase the student's talents in an art project. Although I did this project with middle-school artists, I can envision it being equally exciting for younger students.

Suggested Resource

For some terrific examples of gesture draw-ings, you might check out the drawings of Leonardo da Vinci and Rembrandt van Rijn.

Procedure

1. Unroll enough paper that all students will have a reasonable space to work. (I was able to fit a 30′ length in my classroom.)

2. Arrange students an equal distance apart along one side of the paper, and give each black, red, and white crayons. (You could substitute chalk for the white crayon, as it yields a stronger contrast.)

Sketching a Dancer

Lesson Summary

Students create a collaborative mural of gesture drawings. A *gesture drawing* is a very brief sketch that completely captures the pose or movement of the figure. Gesture drawings frequently serve as the layout sketch for more finished artworks, but they can also be wonderful in themselves.

Purpose

To focus on concepts such as movement and rhythm that are common to both art and dance; to learn gesture drawing skills.

Materials

☐ 3′ wide brown butcher paper

☐ large classroom (or gym or cafeteria)

☐ black, white, and red crayons or chalk

3. Have the dancer dress in a black leotard, white tights, and black dance shoes and position himself or herself a few feet beyond the side of the paper away from the students. You might ask the dancer to hold dance positions briefly or just to dance.

4. Students do as many black-and-white gesture drawings as will fit on their section of paper, overlapping their own sketches and those of their neighbors as necessary. Red is used for occasional emphasis.

When I did this project, Courtney danced for almost the entire period. Music, dance, and drawing merged to yield a work about line, rhythm, movement, repetition, similarity, contrast, shape, form—in short, about music, dance, and drawing. And as the period progressed, the students' respect for Courtney's training, discipline, ability, and stamina grew. The finished mural was quite impressive, unifying the various styles through a common theme (see figure 38).

Figure 38. This mural incorporates gesture drawings of dancer Courtney Krebs.

DRAWING DANCE CLASS

Another possibility is to reverse the preceding procedure by having individual students draw a group of dancers. If you teach in a school that offers dance, this project will be quite simple. It is far more likely that it will require a field trip. In my case, it involved a combined effort on the part of the art and music departments. We arranged to spend a day at the College Conservatory of Music in Cincinnati, Ohio. Your state and local dance centers and universities would probably welcome you as part of their recruiting efforts.

Procedure

Arrange your students in locations that will not interfere with the dancers, and simply allow them to draw throughout the dance class. If you are a dance teacher, you could simply split your class and have one half draw the other as a way to focus on aspects of line, centering, or arm positions.

DANCE SCULPTURES

A nice corollary to this project involves sculpture and the concept of balance. It would be great if you could incorporate a study of correct proportions into this lesson, but this is not vital. Ruth Dorman, an art teacher in California, has had wonderful results from middle-school students who do this project.

Procedure

1. Using one of the drawings from the previous lesson, have each student form a dancing figure out of firm but malleable wire. The focus is not to make a realistic figure, but rather to flesh out the gesture.

2. Once the wire armature (supporting framework) is complete, the student wraps it in tightly crumpled newspaper, securing the layers with masking tape.

3. Then the student covers the whole with papier-mâché or plaster gauze.

4. Once the figure is dry, the student attaches it to a wooden base. For some poses, it might be necessary to create a coat-hanger support and attach that to the wood.

Drawing Dance Class

Lesson Summary

Students create gesture drawings of dancers while observing a dance class.

Purpose

To focus on concepts such as movement and rhythm that are common to both art and dance; to learn gesture drawing skills.

Materials

☐ hard-backed drawing tablets, large clipboards, 12" x 18" pieces of corrugated cardboard, or other sturdy support for drawing on

☐ sketch tablets or several sheets of drawing paper per student

☐ plenty of drawing pencils or crayons

☐ hand-held sharpeners

Dance Sculptures

Lesson Summary

Based on a sketch completed in the previous lesson, each student creates a wire-and-plaster sculpture of a dancer.

Purpose

To focus on concepts common to dance and art; to practice using three-dimensional media.

Materials

- ❑ sturdy but malleable wire (look in hardware stores)
- ❑ crumpled newspaper
- ❑ masking tape
- ❑ papier-mâché or plaster gauze
- ❑ wooden base
- ❑ coat hangers
- ❑ black spray paint and gold tempera or metallic spray paint

Materials tip: It is fairly easy to find scrap wood for the bases at lumberyards and construction sites. I recently purchased a large box of scraps at a hardware store for three dollars. It was being sold as kindling.

5. Allow students to spray the finished piece with metallic spray paint or spray with black spray paint and brush with gold tempera. You can even combine the two paints for a wonderful "bronze" effect.

OTHER DANCE IDEAS

Choreographing dance to a narrative artwork: On a recent trip to New York City, I read an advertisement for a dance company presentation entitled *Guernica*. *Guernica* is a famous mural by Pablo Picasso that memorializes a town destroyed during the Spanish Civil War. It occurred to me that dance teachers have a wonderful way to integrate their discipline with art. There are many narrative paintings and sculptures that could serve as inspirations for choreography! Art and dance classes could work together to create the costumes and sets as well as the story of the piece, or dance students could work on their own. It is fairly easy to project a slide onto the backdrop of a set, and students could either compose a dance or simply improvise movements in an appropriate style or mood. Of course music would be an important aspect of such a lesson, so several disciplines might be united at once.

Artworks relating to dance: A corollary is simply to focus on artworks that relate to dance in some way. The works of Edgar Degas are familiar to almost everyone who has studied ballet, but other artists have treated this subject as well. Once again, you will find references in Egyptian wall paintings, Japanese prints, and Greek vase painting. Pieter Bruegel the Elder painted a piece called *The Wedding Dance,* and Nicolas Poussin created a lovely work entitled *A Dance to the Music of Time. The Dance,* by Henri Matisse, might not be appropriate for all environments, but it is a highly expressive painting.

Drama and Speech

Visual art can be an enormously helpful catalyst in drama and speech classes. Check out the history project on Greek theater masks (page 80) for an activity to coordinate with a study of Classical drama. The chapter on language arts also has several ideas that lend themselves quite readily to dramatic interpretation. For example, the Autobiography lesson (page 108) can easily be adapted to help students develop characters. As I mentioned in my description of the exercise, I originally did it orally. I found that all of the participants somewhat automatically assumed physical traits and speech patterns that fit the persona they had created, and it is easy to see how this idea could be developed to further its dramatic possibilities. Similarly, the idea of using a work of art to inspire creative writing (page 103) is adaptable to theater. One of the exercises we did at the Indianapolis Museum of Art involved posing a group of people in the same positions as figures in a painting. The participants were then asked to pick up the action from that point.

Improvisation to narrative artworks: In a variation of the activity described in the Dance section, works of art such as *Guernica* could inspire either improvisation or scene writing. Scenes or one-act plays could be set "in" works of art and, of course, you could promote research and artistic creativity in the creation of sets, costumes, lighting, and makeup. Perhaps students could be asked to transform themselves into someone from a famous painting. As an added challenge, the painting could be an Expressionist piece, such as Edvard Munch's *The Scream*, or a Cubist work, like Picasso's *Georges Vuillard*.

Theater subjects in artworks: Many artworks have as their subject drama, actors, or actresses. You could easily incorporate these visual aids in your classroom. Everything from illustrations on Greek pottery, Roman mosaics, or Rococo paintings to more modern portraits of well-known performers are possibilities. The Russian-born painter Romain de Tirtoff, better known as Erté, created famous posters based upon his fashion designs for stage and screen. Maurice Sendak, author and illustrator of the children's classic *Where the Wild Things Are*, designs sets and costumes for operas. Al Hirschfeld is famous for his caricatures of Broadway stars. Jean-Antoine Watteau (1684–1721) produced several Rococo paintings of theatrical life, including *Love in the French Theater* and *Love in the Italian Theater*.

Debates about art: Art-related topics make good subjects for both individual presentations and debates and help students understand the issues that confront modern artists. Contemporary culture is rife with questions about the nature of art, the allocation of public funds, what constitutes pornography, the application of First Amendment principles, government support of the arts, and so forth. You may wish to explore the following specific topics:

- When Richard Serra's *Tilted Arc*—a 12-foot-high, 120-foot-long steel wall—was installed at Federal Plaza in New York City in 1981, it stirred enormous controversy about the nature of art, the rights of the artist, and the rights of the public. Each side had legitimate arguments, but ultimately the sculpture was removed. Was this action justified?

- Photographer Robert Mapplethorpe is considered a pornographer by some and a fine artist by others. His work became the focus of a debate about federal funding for the arts when the Corcoran Gallery in Washington, D.C., canceled a show of his photography a few months after his death. The director of the Contemporary Arts Center in Cincinnati, Ohio, was sued for obscenity for presenting the same show. What distinguishes art from pornography? Does a private gallery or museum have the right to display anything it wants? (If you are uncomfortable having your students research this issue, you could provide the pertinent information yourself.)

- The Brooklyn Museum recently mounted a controversial show of contemporary artists, including a painting by Chris Ofili, *The Holy Virgin Mary*, of the Virgin decorated with elephant dung. (According to one source, this is an African device that is in no way demeaning.) Mayor Rudolph Giuliani threatened to withdraw New York City funding for the institution if the exhibit remained. A visitor to the show vandalized the painting by spreading white paint over it. How would your students resolve this issue?

- Bill Gates has purchased the rights to many famous images. The day may come when in order to print an image of the *Mona Lisa* from your computer, you are charged a fee on your credit card. Is this an appropriate use of copyright law?

- Should the government fund the National Endowment for the Arts?

- Over the last twenty-five years, Harold Cohen has created an artificial intelligence system named Aaron that has advanced from drawing simple lines to painting portraits that appear to have been produced by a human being. Using a robotic arm, Aaron does not simply follow Cohen's directions; it makes its own decisions about how to proceed. Is what Aaron makes art? If not, asks Cohen, what is it and how does it differ from the real thing? (To research this topic, simply pop "Harold Cohen's Aaron" into the search engine of your computer and prepare to be amazed!) ❧

References
and Resources

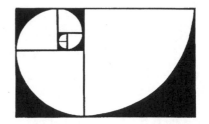

I have divided the resource list into general resource books, many of which are mentioned in part 1, and books on specific topics, which are relevant to the projects described in part 2. I also list a few useful magazines and websites. Finally are lists of videos, filmstrips, and kits, followed by a list of publishers and mail-order companies from which these materials may be obtained. You may wish to request catalogs from some of these companies to assist you in locating other resources.

Works Cited

Anderson, R. L. 1990. *Calliope's Sisters: A Comparative Study of Philosophies of Art.* Englewood Cliffs, N.J.: Prentice Hall.

Bloom, B. J. 1984. *Taxonomy of Educational Objectives: The Classification of Educational Goals.* New York: Longman.

Danto, A. C. 1997. *After the End of Art: Contemporary Art and the Pale of History.* Princeton, N.J.: Princeton University Press.

Feldman, E. B. 1981. *Varieties of Visual Experience.* New York: Harry N. Abrams.

Gabler, N. 1998. *Life, The Movie: How Entertainment Conquered Reality.* New York: Random House.

Gardner, H. 1983. *Frames of Mind: The Theory of Multiple Intelligences.* New York: Basic Books.

Pinkwater, D. 1989. *Fish Whistle.* Reading, Mass.: Addison-Wesley.

Basic Resource Books

Beckett, W. 1994. *The Story of Painting.* New York: Dorling Kindersley.

Bohm-Duchen, M., and J. Cook. 1991. *Understanding Modern Art.* London: Usborne.

Chadwick, W. 1990. *Women, Art, and Society.* London: Thames and Hudson.

Cumming, R. 1995. *Annotated Art.* New York: Dorling Kindersley.

Fleming, W. 1980. *Arts and Ideas.* New York: Holt, Rinehart, and Winston.

Gilbert, R., and W. McCarter. 1985. *Living with Art.* New York: Alfred A. Knopf.

Hume, H. D. 1998. *The Art Teacher's Book of Lists.* Paramus, N.J.: Prentice Hall.

Janson, H. W. 1995. *History of Art.* 5th ed. New York: Harry N. Abrams.

Staniszewski, M. A. 1995. *Believing Is Seeing: Creating the Culture of Art.* New York: Penguin Books.

Strickland, C., and J. Boswell. 1992. *The Annotated Mona Lisa: A Crash Course in Art History from Prehistoric to Post-Modern.* Kansas City, Mo.: Andrews and McMeel.

Tejada, I. 1993. *Brown Bag Ideas from Many Cultures.* Worcester, Mass.: Davis Publications.

Books on Specific Topics

Berrin, K., ed. 1978. *Art of the Huichol Indians.* New York: Harry N. Abrams.

Budge, E. A. W. 1997. *The Dwellers on the Nile: The Life, History, Religion, and Literature of the Ancient Egyptians.* New York: Dover.

Carle, E. 1998. *Hello, Red Fox.* New York: Simon and Schuster.

Fitzpatrick, V. L. 1992. *Art History: A Contextual Inquiry Course.* Reston, Va.: National Art Education Association.

Hansen-Smith, B. 1995. *The Hands-On Marvelous Ball Book.* New York: W. H. Freeman and Co.

Herder, C. V. 1983. *A Leaf Zoo.* Tunbridge Wells, U.K.: Search Press.

Ickis, M. 1949. *The Standard Book of Quilt Making and Collecting.* New York: Dover.

Mather, C. 1990. *Native American Arts, Traditions, and Celebrations.* New York: Crown.

Meshberger, F. L. 1990. "An Interpretation of Michelangelo's *Creation of Adam* Based on Neuroanatomy." *Journal of the American Medical Association* 14:1837–41.

Mexican Art. 1965. The Colour Library of Art Series. London: Paul Hamlyn.

Mikami, T., and J. McDowell. 1961. *The Art of Japanese Brush Painting.* New York: Crown Publishers.

Millington, J. 1989. *Curve Stitching: The Art of Sewing Beautiful Mathematical Patterns.* Stadbroke, U.K.: Tarquin Publications.

Moscovich, I. 1988. *The Magic Cylinder Book: Hidden Pictures to Color and Discover.* Norfolk, U.K.: Tarquin Publications.

Mottershead, L. 1977. *Metamorphosis: A Sourcebook of Mathematical Discovery.* Palo Alto, Calif.: Dale Seymour.

Pappas, T. 1999. *Mathematical Footprints: Discovering Mathematical Impressions All Around Us.* San Carlos, Calif.: Wide World Publishing/Tetra.

Parrinder, G., ed. 1982. *African Mythology.* Rev. ed. London: Paul Hamlyn.

Pickover, C. A. 1997. *The Loom of God: Mathematical Tapestries at the End of Time.* New York: Plenum Press

Schneider, M. S. 1994. *A Beginner's Guide to Constructing the Universe: The Mathematical Archetypes of Nature, Art, and Science.* New York: HarperCollins.

Segy, L. 1976. *Masks of Black Africa.* New York: Dover.

Serra, M. 1997. *Discovering Geometry: An Inductive Approach.* Berkeley, Calif.: Key Curriculum Press.

Shlain, L. 1991. *Art and Physics: Parallel Visions in Space, Time, and Light.* New York: William Morrow.

Spiegelman, A. 1973. *Maus: A Survivor's Tale*. Vol. 1: *My Father Bleeds History*. New York: Pantheon Books.

Sullivan, C., ed. 1994. *Here Is My Kingdom: Hispanic-American Literature and Art for Young People*. New York: Harry N. Abrams.

Taylor, C. F., ed. 1994. *Native American Myths and Legends*. London: Salamander Books.

Ting, F. 1990. *Chinese Painting*. New York: Dover.

Valadez, M., and S. Valadez. 1992. *Huichol Indian Sacred Rituals*. Oakland, Calif.: Dharma Enterprises.

Willson, J. 1983. *Mosaic and Tessellated Patterns: How to Create Them*. New York: Dover.

Magazines

Arts and Activities
591 Camino de la Reina, Suite 200
San Diego, CA 92108
www.artsandactivities.com

Scholastic, Inc. (Art)
555 Broadway
New York, N.Y 10012
800-387-1437 ext. 99
www.scholastic.com

School Arts
50 Portland St.
Worcester, MA 01608
800-533-2847
www.davis-art.com (go to "School Arts Magazine")

Websites

Art Becomes the Fourth R: http://jasonohler.com

Artcyclopedia: http://www.artcyclopedia.com/about.html

Artsednet: http://www.artsednet.getty.edu/ArtsEdNet/

4Art: http://4art.4anything.com/

The Getty Center for Education in the Arts: http://www.getty/edu/

Marc Frantz: http://www.math.iupui.edu/mtc/Art/Art.html

National Art Education Association: http://www.naea-reston.org/

Sycamore School Art Department: http://www.sycamoreschool.org/specials/art/art.html

Web Gallery of Art: http://gallery.euroweb.hu/index1.html

Webmuseum: http://sunsite.dcc.uchile.cl/wm/

Videos, Filmstrips, and Kits

African American Art: Past and Present. 3-part series. 1992. Wilton, Conn.: Reading and O'Reilly. [video]

African Art and Culture. 1993. Chicago, Ill.: Clearvue/eav. [video]

Ancient Greek Art and Architecture. 1982. History through Art and Architecture Series. Boulder, Colo.: Alarion Press. [filmstrip]

Ancient Roman Art and Architecture. 1982. History through Art and Architecture Series Boulder, Colo.: Alarion Press. [filmstrip]

Art Is . . . Basic Perspective Drawing. n.d. By G. Brommer. Single Concepts in Art Series. Aspen Colo.; Glenview, Ill.: Crystal Video. [video]

The Art of the Dogon. 1988. New York: Metropolitan Museum of Art. [video]

Art of Japan. 1982. Oriental Art Series. Wilton, Conn.: Reading and O'Reilly. [filmstrip]

The Art of Mexico, Central America, and South America. 1993. By L. D. Rosenfeld. Walch Multicultural Art Series. Portland, Maine: J. Weston Walch. [video]

Chinese Art and Architecture. 1987. History through Art and Architecture Series. Boulder, Colo.: Alarion Press. [filmstrip]

Chinese Painting. 1982. Oriental Art Series. Wilton, Conn.: Reading and O'Reilly. [filmstrip]

Cuentos de las Fibres: Stories of the Yarns. 1991. Gente del Sol Series. Tucson, Ariz.: Crizmac. [filmstrip]

Daimyo. 1988. Washington, D.C.: National Gallery of Art. [video]

Daughters of the Anasazi. 1990. Washington, D.C.: U.S. Department of the Interior, Indian Arts and Crafts Board. [video]

Egyptian Art and Architecture. 1982. History through Art and Architecture Series. Boulder, Colo.: Alarion Press. [filmstrip]

Huichol Indians of Mexico: A Culture Kit. 1990. Oakland, Calif.: Ethnic Arts and Facts. [kit]

Masters of Illusion. 1991. Washington, D.C.: National Gallery of Art. [video]

Nôtre Dame, Cathedral of Amiens. Part 1: *Reflections—Live Walk Through* and Part 2: *Revelation—Computer and Architectural Animation.* 1997. Amiens Trilogy. Aspen Colo.: Glenview, Ill.: Crystal Productions. [three-video set]

Renaissance Art and Architecture. 1982. History through Art and Architecture Series. Boulder, Colo.: Alarion Press. [filmstrip]

Sacred Ground: The Story of the American Indian and His Relationship to the Land. 1977. Los Angeles: Freewheelin' Films. [video]

Touching the Timeless. 1992. The Millennium Series. PBS. [video]

Tribal Design. 1988. Tucson, Ariz.: Crizmac. [filmstrips]

World Folk Art: A Multicultural Approach. 1991. Aspen, Colo.; Glenview, Ill.: Crystal Productions. [videos]

Publishers and Mail-Order Companies

Alarion Press
P.O. Box 1882
Boulder, CO 80306
800-523-9177
www.alarion.com

Clearvue/eav
6465 N. Avondale Ave.
Chicago, IL 60631
800-253-2788
www.clearvue.com

Crizmac
P.O. Box 65928
Tucson, AZ 85728
800-913-8555
www.crizmac.com

Crystal Productions
P.O. Box 2159
Glenview, IL 60025
800-255-8629
www.crystalproductions.com

Davis Publications
50 Portland St.
Worcester, MA 01608
800-533-2847 ext. 254
www.davis-art.com

Dick Blick Art Materials
P.O. Box 1267
Galesburg, IL 61401
800-447-8192
www.dickblick.com

Dover Publications
31 E. Second St.
Mineola, NY 11501
516-294-7000
http://
store.doverpublications.com

Ethnic Arts and Facts
P.O. Box 20550
Oakland, CA 94620
510-465-0451
www.ethnicartsnfacts.com

Media for the Arts
73 Pelham St.
Newport, RI 02840
800-554-6008
www.art-history.com

Nasco Arts and Crafts
901 Janesville Ave.
Ft. Atkinson, WI 53538
or
P.O. Box 3837
Modesto, CA 95352
800-558-9595
www.nascofa.com

Sax Arts and Crafts
2405 S. Calhoun Rd.
P.O. Box 51710
New Berlin, WI 53151
800-558-9595
www.artsupplies.com

**Shorewood Fine Art
Reproductions**
33 River Rd.
Cos Cob, CT 06807
www.artforschools.com

Triarco Arts and Crafts
14650 28th Ave.
North Plymouth, MN 55447
800-328-3360
e-mail:
info@triarcoarts.com

**United Art and Education
(Art Materials Catalog)**
P.O. Box 9219
Fort Wayne, IN 46899
800-858-3247
www.UnitedNow.com

Universal Color Slide Co.
8450 S. Tamiami Trail
Sarasota, FL 34238
800-326-1367

University Prints
21 East St.
Winchester, MA 01890
781-729-8006
www.universityprints.net

Index

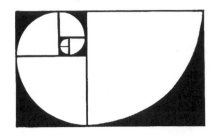

About the Author

Eileen Prince has been an art specialist in Indianapolis-area schools since 1970. The art curriculum she designed has won recognition on both local and national levels. Her work appears in art collections both here and abroad. Eileen holds a master's degree with distinction in art education from Herron School of Art/Indiana University. Her accomplishments have been recognized in *Outstanding Young Women of America (1974)* and *Who's Who in American Education (1996-97)*. She has served as a consultant to a variety of individual teachers and school corporations and speaks frequently at workshops and conferences.

Encourage and Enhance Your Students' Independent Thinking Skills!

INVENTING TOYS

Kids Having Fun Learning Science
by Ed Sobey, Ph.D.

Grades 4–8   ISBN: 1-56976-124-8

Ed Sobey brings his joy of inventing to this easy-to-use book of innovative hands-on activities. Find out why critics everywhere call his books **"valuable"** *(Booklist)*, **"refreshing"** *(Library Journal)*, **"recommended"** *(US News and World Report)*, and full of **"creativity and ingenuity"** *(Children's Literature)*.

In *Inventing Toys,* Sobey has transformed *learning* science and math concepts into creative, stimulating adventures to enable kids to *do* science in the classroom and at home. Your students will invent toys using these hands-on activities, and you'll be able to monitor your students' progress in meeting benchmarks and National Science Education Standards. *Inventing Toys* makes it easy to teach through creative problem-solving and to tie inventing adventures to your science curriculum. The six workshops—including building toy cars, toy boats, and pneumatic-blast rockets—were classroom-tested to enthusiastic response. One fifth-grade student described her workshop as the **"best day in school, ever."**

Soft Cover, 144 pages
1121-W . . . $23.00

SMART ART

Learning to Classify and Critique Art
by Patricia Hollingsworth and Stephen Hollingsworth

Grades 3–8   ISBN: 0-913705-31-4

You can learn along with your class as you introduce your students to the world of art. With *Smart Art* your students will classify and critique art, enhance thinking skills, acquire art vocabulary, and develop aesthetic understanding.

This discipline-based program includes more than 35 black-and-white and 4 full-color art reproductions. The 75 hands-on art activities that accompany the reproductions develop thinking, drawing, and writing skills. It's all here for the teacher—reproducible workbook pages, in-depth art background, teacher's guide, and a complete glossary of art vocabulary.

Soft cover, 112 pages
1009-W . . . $25.00

Order Form

Qty.	Item #	Title	Unit Price	Total
	1121-W	Inventing Toys	$23	
	1009-W	Smart Art	$25	

Name _____

Address _____

City _____

State _____ Zip _____

Phone (_____) _____

E-mail _____

Method of payment (check one):

❑ Check or Money Order   ❑ Visa

❑ MasterCard   ❑ Purchase Order Attached

Credit Card No. _____

Expires _____

Signature _____

Subtotal	
Sales Tax (AZ residents, 5.6%)	
S & H (10% of subtotal–min $5.50)	
Total (U.S. funds only)	

CANADA: add 30% for S & H and G.S.T.

☎

Please include your phone number in case we have questions about your order.

Call, write, e-mail, or FAX for your FREE catalog!

P.O. Box 66006-W
Tucson, AZ 85728-6006

1-800-232-2187
520-322-5090
FAX 520-323-9402
neways2learn@zephyrpress.com

└ — Order these resources and more any time, day or night, online at **www.zephyrpress.com** or **www.i-home-school.com** — ┘